# The Tales
## of
# Rabbi Nachman

# MARTIN BUBER

# THE TALES
# OF
# RABBI NACHMAN

translated from the German by
**Maurice Friedman**

with a new Introduction by
**Paul Mendes-Flohr**

Professor of Modern Jewish Thought
The Hebrew University of Jerusalem

and

**Ze'ev Gries**

Lecturer in Jewish Mysticism and Hasidism,
The Hebrew University of Jerusalem

HUMANITIES PRESS INTERNATIONAL, INC.
Atlantic Highlands, NJ

This edition first published with a new introduction and
appendix, 1988 in the United States of America by
HUMANITIES PRESS INTERNATIONAL, INC., Atlantic
Highlands, NJ 07716

**Library of Congress Cataloging-in-Publication Data**

Buber, Martin, 1878–1965.
    [Geschichten des Rabbi Nachman.   English]
    The tales of Rabbi Nachman / [adapted by] Martin Buber;
translated from the German by Maurice Friedman; with a new
introduction by Paul Mendes-Flohr and Ze'ev Gries.
      p.  cm.
    Translation of: Die Geschichten des Rabbi Nachman.
    Adaptation of: Sipure-ma'asiyot / Naḥman of Bratslav.
    Reprint. Originally published: New York: Horizon Press,
1956. With new introd.
    Bibliography: p.
    ISBN 0–391–03548–7 (pbk.): $15.00 (est.)
    1. Parables, Hasidic.   I. Naḥman, of Bratslav, 1772–1811.
Sipure
ma'asiyot.  II. Title.
BM532.B77513 1988
833' .912—dc19                                      87–22906
                                                       CIP

Printed in the United States of America

# CONTENTS

Foreword    vii

Introduction    ix

## Rabbi Nachman and Jewish Mysticism

Jewish Mysticism    3

Rabbi Nachman of Bratzlav    19

Sayings of Rabbi Nachman    35

The Stories    43

## The Tales of Rabbi Nachman

The Rabbi and His Son    49

The Steer and the Ram    59

The Clever Man and the Simple Man    71

The King's Son and the Son of the Maid    95

The Master of Prayer    115

The Seven Beggars    149

# Rabbi Nachman's Journey to Palestine

Rabbi Nachman's Journey to Palestine      179

# Appendix      215

# FOREWORD

My re-creation of the tales of Rabbi Nachman first appeared in print fifty years ago. I have not translated these tales, but retold them with full freedom, yet out of his spirit as it is presented to me.

The tales have been preserved for us in the notes of a disciple, notes that have obviously deformed and distorted the original narrative beyond measure. As they lie before us, they appear confused, verbose, and ignoble in form. I have been at pains to preserve unchanged all the elements of the fables that convinced me through their power and colorfulness that they are a part of the original.

In the preliminary part of this book I have sought to present the atmosphere of the whole. The section that I have entitled *Jewish Mysticism* is to be regarded, accordingly, as only a first and very general introduction to that subject.

Martin Buber
*Jerusalem, 1956*

# INTRODUCTION

With the publication in 1906 of *The Tales of Rabbi Nachman* (*Die Geschichten des Rabbi Nachman*),[1] Buber introduced the educated German and Western public to the mystical wisdom and spiritual nobility of Hasidism, the movement of popular mysticism that arose in the eighteenth century among the Jews of Poland and the Ukraine. The first of many works Buber was to publish on Hasidism, this gracefully written and elegantly produced volume—designed in accordance with the finest standards of the then fasionable *Jugendstil*[2]—disclosed the remarkable spiritual universe of the hitherto despised Hasidim, as the votaries of the movement are called. For the educated European—Jew and non-Jew alike—the Hasidim had been an emblem of religious superstition and backwardness, denizens, as the Austrian Jewish writer Karl Ermil Franzos (1848–1904) derisively observed, of "Semi-Asia" (*Halb-Asien*).[3] In the eyes of many educated Europeans the Hasidim epitomized the *Ostjuden*—the unenlightened residents of the vast "Oriental" ghetto of Eastern Europe, obdurately beholden to an allegedly anachronistic faith burdened by religious formalism and a legalistic conception of one's service to God. Indeed, Hasidism came to characterize the negative image of Judaism prevailing in Western culture. Thus, by highlighting the spiritual verve and imagination of Hasidism, Buber also served to restore a respect for Judaism.[4]

Buber rendered Hasidism respectable, as it were, by integrating this most distinctive manifestation of East European Jewish spirituality into the general discourse and idiom of fin de siècle intellectual fashion, namely, the New Romanticism (and later, Expressionism). In his presentation of Hasidism, Buber would thus subtly and favorably compare its spiritual sensibility with that of other mystical traditions—specifically, those sponsored by medieval Christianity and various Oriental religions—honored by the New Romanticism. Buber also presented Hasidism in terms of its legends and myths—expressions of pre-Enlightenment folk wisdom. These the publisher Eugen Diederichs (1867–1930), the Maecenas of the New Romanticism, celebrated as capturing an intuitive and therefore, in his judgment, genuine metaphysical experience of the world's primal unity, which, alas, the regnant bourgeois civilization, with its divisive ethos and analytical intellect, had obfuscated.[5] Hasidism, Buber boldly asserted, is also founded on an apprehension of the world's primal unity and thus it—and the millennial mystical tradition from whence it emerged, Kabbala—is uniquely relevant to the concerns of the educated individual bound by the spiritual quest of the fin de siècle.

Upon publishing *The Tales of Rabbi Nachman*, Buber sent a copy to Diederichs, and in the accompanying letter he recalled a conversation several years earlier when the publisher had doubted whether Judaism, which he deemed to be utterly bereft of spontaneity and inwardness, could provide the soil for mysticism:[6]

> You perhaps recall our conversation of several years ago when we discussed the question of the existence of a Jewish mysticism. You did not at all want to believe it. With the Nachman-book I have initiated a series documenting the existence of a Jewish mysticism.

Buber was fully cognizant that Diederichs' doubts about Judaism's capacity for mysticism expressed a prevailing prejudice. And he undoubtedly had such prejudice in mind when, in the very first paragraph to his Nachman book, he declared that Rabbi Nachman of Bratslav—"perhaps the last Jewish mystic"—"stands at the end of an unbroken tradition whose beginning we do not know. For a long time men sought to deny this tradition; today it can no longer be doubted."[7] Furthermore, Buber observed, this tradition "is one of the great manifestations of ecstatic wisdom." To be sure, Jewish mysticism bears the influence of other mystical traditions, but, Buber emphasized, "the tendency toward mysticism is native to the Jews from antiquity. [Indeed], the strength of Jewish mysticism was drawn from an original characteristic of the people that produced it." In his next work on Hasidism, *The Legends of the Baal Shem* (*Die Legende des Baal Schem*), Buber would make a similar point when he asserted apodictically that "the Jews are perhaps the only people that has never ceased to produce myth. . . , [and Hasidism] is the latest form of Jewish myth that we know."[8]

Buber's early pronouncements on Hasidism constituted a profound challenge to the prevailing opinion among enlightened Europeans regarding the nature of Jewish spirituality. Somewhat ironically, the acculturated Jews of the West, as Gershom Scholem observed, shared this opinion, and deliberately "excluded and repudiated" mysticism and myth from their conception of Judaism.[9] And no one, Scholem noted, deserved "more credit for first causing these features of Judaism to come to view again than Buber . . ." A piquant but poignant insight into the resistance of the enlightened Jew to Buber's efforts to rehabilitate the image of Hasidism and to rescue from oblivion expressions of Jewish mystical piety is provided by a letter, dated 6 February 1908, to Buber from his father Carl (1848–1935), a successful Austrian businessman:[10]

Dear Martin,
Please receive my most heartfelt wishes for your birthday: May
your work bring you the success you desire and may your life be
free of care and worry.

    I would be happy were you to give up this hasidic and Zohar
stuff [i.e., mysticism], for it could only have a mentally debasing
and pernicious effect. It is a pity to devote your talents to such a
fruitless subject, and to waste so much time and effort [on some-
thing] so utterly useless for yourself and the world.

    The attitude of his grandfather, Salomon Buber
(1827–1906), on the other hand, was more encour-
aging. This distinguished scholar of Midrash, who
actually raised his grandson in his home in Lemberg
(Lvov), in Austrian Galicia, took an active interest in
his work, and provided him with Hasidic texts un-
available in Berlin.[11] Just before his death in Decem-
ber 1906, Salomon Buber received a copy of *The Tales
of Rabbi Nachman*, and the dedication it bore undoubtedly pleased him exceedingly: "To my grandfather
Salomon Buber, the last master of the old *haskalah*, I
dedicate this work on Hasidism with reverence and
love."[12]

    In preparing his first studies on Hasidism, Buber
also enjoyed the support of several East European scholars, particularly Michah Yosef Berdyczewski (1865–
1921), Simon Dubnow (1860–1941) and Samuel A.
Horodezky (1871–1957),[13] who had already written
treatises—in Hebrew, Yiddish and Russian—on various aspects of Hasidism and Kabbala. In contrast to

their scholarly interest in Hasidism, Buber's was neither that of a historian nor that of a philologist. "It is not at all my intention to collect new facts," Buber explained to Horodetzky in a letter dated July 1906, "but simply to provide a new understanding [*Auffassung*] of Jewish mysticism and its interconnections, to give a new synthetic presentation of [this tradition] and its creations, and to make these creations known to a European public in as artistically pure a form as possible."[14] He therefore decided not to translate these creations—the legends and allegorical tales related by the Hasidic masters—but rather to "retell" (*nacherzaehlen*) them. Selecting various motifs from Hasidic stories that, in his judgment, captured the distinctive message of Hasidism, Buber would "relive" (*nacherleben*) these motifs and the message they conveyed, retelling them as he experienced (*erleben*) them.

Before having set upon this approach to unlocking the message—or what today might be called the kerygmatic core—of the Hasidic tales and legends, Buber had, in fact, initially sought to translate them and was recurrently frustrated by a seemingly intractable problem. As recorded in Hebrew by the often uneducated followers of the Hasidic masters, who related their tales and legends orally in Yiddish, the material Buber had to work with was linguistically "crude and ungainly," and as such obfuscated the spiritual "purity" animating the tales.[15] In an essay

from 1918, "My Way to Hasidism," Buber recalled
his initial and unsuccessful efforts to translate the
Hasidic tales directly into German:[16]

I noted that the [spiritual] purity [of the original Hasidic tales and
legends] did not allow itself to be preserved in translation, much
less enhanced—I had to tell the stories that I had taken *into*
myself, as a true painter takes into himself the lines of the models
and achieves the genuine images out of the memory formed of
them. . . . And, therefore, although by far the largest part of [my
early work on Hasidism] is autonomous fiction composed from the
traditional motifs, I might honestly report of my experience of the
legend: I bore in my blood the spirit of those who created it, and
out of my blood and spirit it has become new.

Buber's decision not to translate but rather to retell
the Hasidic tales was, therefore, not prompted by
mere aesthetic considerations; his motive was primarily
methodological. His friend and mentor in the study of
mystical texts, Gustav Landauer (1870–1919) encountered a similar methodological problem in rendering the sermons of the thirteenth-century German
Dominican monk, Meister Eckhart, from medieval
into modern German. In the prospectus to his 1903
anthology, *Meister Eckharts Mystische Schriften* (The
Mystical Writings of Meister Eckhart), Landauer noted
that the volume seeks "the return of a lost individual
—an individual who is not to be historically appre-
ciated, but filled [anew] with life."[17] One who seeks to
retrieve the person and teachings of a great master

from the obscurity imposed by the passage of time should not render the texts whereby the these teachings were transmitted literally into a more contemporary language, but requicken for the reader the *Erlebnis* (experience) that gave birth to those teachings. Buber concurred. In the introduction to his highly acclaimed collection of mystical testimonies, *Ecstatic Confessions* (*Ekstatische Konfessionen*)—published by Eugen Diederichs in 1909—Buber succinctly explained the principles of his selection and rendition: "The ecstatic individual may be explained in terms of psychology, physiology, pathology; what is important to us is that which remains beyond explanation: the individual's experience (*Erlebnis*). We pay no heed here to those notions which are bent on establishing 'order' even in the darkest corners; we are listening to a human being speak the soul and the soul's ineffable mystery."[18]

For Landauer and Buber, the translation of works of the spirit derived from the past was preeminently a hermeneutical task, which followed an axis of *Erlebnis* (lived experience) and *Nacherleben* (re-experiencing). This conception reflects the influence of *Lebensphilosophie* (philosophy of life), in particular the hermeneutical doctrines of Wilhelm Dilthey (1833–1911), with whom Buber had studied in Berlin at the turn at the century, and whom, after an elapse of more than fifty years, he still referred to as "my teacher."[19] Dilthey placed the twin categories of *Er-*

*lebnis* and *Nacherleben* at the center of the *Geistes-wissenschaften* (humanities and social sciences) and his account of the creative process. In one of his earliest programmatic essays, Dilthey spoke of "the constant translation of lived-experience into form and form into lived-experience"[20]; *Erlebnis* is the ground of the creative act that is "objectified" in the varied expressions of the human spirit—such as poetry, art, monuments, institutions, and religious and philosophical systems—and hence the ability to relive the founding *Erlebnis* of any given spiritual expression is the ontological nexus between the past and the present, allowing for the retrieval of the past as an abiding "presence" in the present. As Hans Gadamer, who elaborated Dilthey's teachings into a systematic theory of hermeneutics, was later to observe the hermeneutic task is preeminently a matter of mediating the past and the present, of retrieving the meaning (*Bedeutung*) borne by the creations of the human spirit or *Erlebnisaus-druecke* (expressions of the lived experience) bequeathed to us from the past. Hermeneutics, Gadamer declared in a language that betrays the influence not only of Dilthey but also apparently of Buber,[21]

is not concerned primarily with the amassing of ratified knowledge which satisfies the methodological ideal of science—yet is concerned, here too, with knowledge and truth. In understanding tradition not only are texts understood, but insights are gained and truths acknowledged. . . . The experience of the "Thou" also manifests the paradoxical element that something standing over against me asserts its own rights and requires absolute recognition; and in that very process is "understood." . . . This understanding does not at all understand the "Thou," but what the "Thou" truly says to us.

Buber would actually develop his own conception of hermeneutics as a dialogue between the present and the past, as embodied in a text, only in the period subsequent to the publication of *The Tales of Rabbi Nachman*, and in particular after having crystallized his philosophy of dialogue to which he gave his first expression in *I and Thou* (1923). But clearly there is a continuity between his dialogical and earlier hermeneutical endeavors as represented by *The Tales of Rabbi Nachman*.

Buber was later to acknowledge that in these his earliest efforts he was somewhat over-eager to render the Hasidic tales susceptible to the aesthetic sensibility of the contemporary Western reader, and thus tended to overextend poetic license in an attempt to free the essential message of Hasidism from what he felt to be the alien and unappealing idiom of the original:[22]

I did not listen attentively enough to . . . the living folk-tone which could be heard from within this material. At work in me here, too, was a natural' reaction against the attitude of most Jewish historians of the nineteenth century toward Hasidism, in which they found nothing but wild superstition. The need, in the face of this misunderstanding, to point out the purity and loftiness of Hasid-

ism led me to pay all too little attention to its popular vitality. . . .
The representation of the Hasidic teaching that I gave in [my
earliest works] was essentially faithful; but where I retold the legendary tradition, I still did so just as the Western author that I was.

Although Buber may have indeed neglected to convey
the flavor of the original texts, the hermeneutical
difficulties that confronted him should not be mini-
mized. To translate the texts literally might preserve
their quaint, folk quality, but perhaps at the price of
obscuring for the Western reader what Buber perceived to be their founding *Erlebnis* and pristine spiritual message. In a letter to the Hungarian literary
critic Georg Lukács (1885–1971), Buber succinctly
articulated his understanding of the hermeneutical
problem he confronted. An ardent admirer of *The
Tales of Rabbi Nachman* and *The Legends of the Baal
Shem*, Lukacs wrote Buber from Florence in November 1911,[23] expressing his

deep gratitude for your two books, *Baal Shem* and *Rabbi Nachman*, which due to circumstances I was only able to read this
summer. . . . It is only a pity that [the volumes are] so slim; it is
hardly possible, after all, that this is all that remains. Is there any
sort of (German, French or English) edition which is more complete? Or will you yourself, my dear Doctor, decide all the same to
prepare a larger edition? I should think, as in the case the Indian
texts, it may not be possible to put a complete edition together?
There is so much—for example, the ethical aspects of the trans-
migration of the soul—that one would be glad to learn about
within the whole extent of the tradition.

*xix*

Buber was obviously perplexed but, nonetheless, replied in a forthright manner:[24]

That you found my "Chassidica" satisfying, I was very happy to hear. I must confess (I cannot keep it from you)—and I hope that your feelings for the work will not be negatively affected—that in the *Baal Shem* the innermost motifs alone are "authentic." I refer to the stories only, naturally, since the sayings quoted in the foreword are exact translations of the original.

The same is true of the last two tales of *Nachman*. For this reason, you can see why a collection of texts as you envision is such a tricky affair. I could, I suppose, put together a slim volume of aphorisms—I have, indeed, given it some thought [25]—but the bulk of the text of the stories would yield certain motifs only. Should you come to Berlin (when will that be?) I will do an on-the-spot literal translation of a few texts for you. You will then have a better understanding of my attitude. . .

An examination of the texts that Buber had in mind would bear out his contention. The texts transmitted to us are indeed confounded and corrupted; they cannot be taken as a *verbatim* record of the tales and legends related by the Hasidic masters. Current historical research and scholarly analysis of the Hasidic literature indicate that the masters, including Nachman of Bratzlav, delivered their sermons, which contained tales and legends, in Yiddish and principally during the *seudah shlishit*, the so-called "third meal" when toward the conclusion of the Sabbath, the Hasidim would gather at the master's *tisch* (table) to "dine" and discuss Torah with him. Since the "meal" and the master's accompanying sermon were largely during the Sabbath, writing was forbidden. Further, the masters certainly did not write out their sermons beforehand. Scribes would then have transcribed the sermons they heard after the Sabbath, apparently rendering them, although usually delivered in Yiddish, immediately into Hebrew—a language they rarely knew as well as they knew Yiddish but which they found to be a vessel more appropriate to the dignity and the holiness of the words of their venerated masters. The Hebrew of these scribes, alas, was a confused mixture of biblical, rabbinic, and medieval Hebrew, employed with no particular logic and following the syntax of Yiddish; orthographical and grammatical errors also abounded. From the literary point of view, the result is a singularly infelicitous literature. Accordingly, the problems that Buber spoke of in his letter to Lukács and elsewhere were no contrivance or figment of his imagination; the kerygmatic core—or primal message—of the Hasidic story and legend, grounded in a founding *Erlebnis* and uttered orally in Yiddish by the Hasidic masters, is buried in written documents that seem to garble the original utterances in an often ungainly and confused Hebrew translation. Surely, given the hermeneutical and literary task he set for himself, to present the Hasidic kerygma in an accessible and aesthetically pleasing manner, confronted Buber with an enormous challenge.[26]

When one examines Buber's papers at the Martin
Buber Archive in Jerusalem, one is struck by the
incredible amount of Hasidic literature he read and
transcribed, often translating literally passages of
various length. An edifying example is a passage from
*Likkutei Moharan*, a collection of Nachman of Bratzlav's teachings. In section 133, of which (in the docu-
ment found in his archive) Buber copied in Hebrew
the last lines, he added a literal German translation,
whereas in *The Tales of Rabbi Nachman* he presented
a stylized rendition of the entire passage. In the original the text reads literally:

Like a small coin, if you should hold it before your eyes it will
prevent [you] from seeing a big mountain. . . . But one can easily
remove the coin from one's eyes and one will immediately see the
big mountain before one. . . . And so I heard in the name of the
Besht [the Baal Shem Tov, the founder of Hasidism] the following: Woe, the world is full of wondrous and awesome lights and
mysteries, and a little hand stands before the eyes and prevents
one from beholding the great lights.

In his notes Buber translated the concluding citation
from the Besht: "Woe, the world is full of powerful
lights and mysteries, and man conceals them with his
little hand" ("Wehe, die Welt ist voll gewaltigen Lichten
und Geheimnisse, und der Mensch verstellt sie sich mit
seiner kleinen Hand."[27]) In *The Tales of Rabbi Nachman*, Buber presents the entire passage thus:[28]

As the hand held before the eye conceals the greatest mountain, so the little earthly life hides from the glance of the enormous lights and mysteries of which the world is full, and he who can draw it away from before his eyes, as one draws away a hand, beholds the great shining of the inner worlds.

Note how Buber in his rendition condensed and aestheticized the original and, incidentally, conflated the words of the Besht cited by Rabbi Nachman—the very passage he had translated literally in his notes—with those of Rabbi Nachman himself. Buber would justify this rendition hermeneutically, indicating that he is merely interested in preserving the principal motif and kerygmatic message of the said passage.

Throughout his lifelong interest in Hasidism, Buber often consulted with scholars and knowledgeable observers of the movement. While working on *The Tales of Rabbi Nachman,* as noted, he enjoyed the active support of various scholars, namely, Berdyczewski, Dubnow, Horodezky, and especially his grandfather, Salomon Buber. Indeed, throughout his life, Buber would often consult with knowledgeable observers of the movement, ever eager to gain new insights and bibliographical references. The correspondence, stretching over a period of more than fifty years, between Buber and the novelist Shemuel Yoseph Agnon (1888–1970), will soon be published in Hebrew. Agnon, born in Galicia, was intimate with Hasidism and shared with Buber a deep affection for the movement. Together Buber and Agnon planned to edit and issue a comprehensive compendium of Hasidic sources to be called *Corpus Chassidicum*. They had already collected considerable material when in 1924 a fire swept Agnon's residence in Bad Homburg, a suburb of Frankfurt, and destroyed the books and notes. Although they never resumed the project, Agnon and Buber continued to exchange Hasidic bibliography and, especially, tales and anecdotes. One charming example of their correspondence will suffice. In a letter of 17 October 1916, Agnon added a postscript:[29]

In order not to leave any blank space I will relate to you a lovely anecdote. "When the hasidim of Rabbi Dov of Mezeritsch would crowd in upon him, diverting him from the Torah and divine devotion, he would say. 'If you will continue to crowd in upon me so, soon you will not have to whom to come.'"

This anecdote was undoubtedly part of the ongoing oral tradition of Hasidism, which through the good offices Agnon and other friends Buber tirelessly collected till his death in June 1965. In ordering his voluminous papers, the director of the Martin Buber Archive and former personal secretary, Margot Cohen, came across and identified thirteen sayings (*Lehrworte*) from Rabbi Nachman not included in previous editions of *The Tales of Rabbi Nachman*. These sayings are here published in an appendix.[30]

# NOTES

1. First translated from the German in 1956 by Maurice Friedman and published by Horizon Press, New York; subsequently republished in 1962 by Indiana University Press, and in 1970 by Avon Press of New York.

2. The initialing, for instance, was executed by the renowned *Jugendstil* artist Emil Rudolof Weiss (1875–1942). On Buber's attention to the aesthetic details of his publications and its significance for an understanding of his work, see Mendes-Flohr, *Von der Mystik zum Dialog. Martin Buber's geistige Entwicklung bis hin zu "Ich und Du."* (Koenigstein a/T: Juedischer Verlag, 1976), pp. 112–14.

3. Franzos first used the term *Halb-Asien* in his collection of tales of East European life, in which sketches of the Jewish ghetto figure most prominently: *Aus Halb-Asien. Kulturbilder aus Galizien, der Bukowina, Suedrussland und Rumaenien* (Stuttgart/Berlin, 1876), 2 vols. He used the term *Halb-Asien* often in his writings, applying it rather indiscriminately to all those lands that lie "nicht bloss geographisch, sondern auch in ihrem Kulturleben zwischen dem gebildeten Europa und dem barbarischen Asien." Franzos, *Von Don zur Donau* (Stuttgart/Berlin, 1878), II, 193.

4. On the negative image of Judaism as an alien Asiatic religion and Buber's contribution to the rehabilitation of this image, see Mendes-Flohr, "Fin-de-Siècle Orientalism, the Ostjuden and the Aesthetics of Jewish Self-Affirmation," in Jonathan Frankel, ed., *Studies in Contemporary Judaism* (Bloomington: Indiana University Press, 1982), pp. 96–138.

5. On Diederichs and his Weltanschauung, see W. G. Oschilewski, *Eugen Diederichs und sein Werk* (Jena: Eugen Diederichs Verlag, 1936); also E. Diederichs, *Aus meinem Leben* (Jena: Eugen Diederichs Verlag, 1938).

6. Buber an Diederichs, 21 January 1907, Buber, *Briefwechsel aus sieben Jahrzehnten*, ed. Grete Schaeder (Heidelberg: Verlag Lambert Schneider, 1972), I, 253f. Diederichs' attitude toward Judaism is discussed in George Mosse, *The Crisis of German Ideology. Intellectual Origins of the Third Reich* (New York: Grosset & Dunlap, 1964), pp. 57f.

7. *The Tales of Rabbi Nachman*, p. 3.

8. *Legends of the Baal Shem*, trans. M. Friedman (New York: Schocken Books, 1969), pp. xi, xiii.

9. "Martin Buber's conception of Judaism," in Scholem, *On Jews and Judaism in Crisis. Selected Essays*, trans. W. J. Dannhauser (New York: Schocken, 1976), p. 142.

10. *Briefwechsel*, I, 260f.

11. See, for example, Salomon Buber to Martin Buber, letter dated 26 November 1906, *Briefwechsel*, I, 248.

12. After his grandfather's death, Buber changed the dedication in subsequent printings and editions to read: "Dem Gedaechtnis meines Grossvaters Salomon Buber des letzten Meisters der alten Haskala bringe ich in Treuen dies Werk der Chassidut dar"—"In the memory of my grandfather, the last master of the old *haskalah*, I offer with devotion this work on Hasidism."

13. Buber consulted with each of these scholars, whose assistance he acknowledged in the preface to the first edition of *Die Geschichten des Rabbi Nachman*. Also see Buber's correspondence with Dubnow and Horodezky in *Briefwechsel*, I, 252f., 244, 263f.

14. *Briefwechsel*, I, 244f.

15. "Hasidism and Modern Man," in Buber, *Hasidism and Modern Man*, trans. M. Friedman, intro. Martin Jaffee (Atlantic Highlands, New Jersey: Humanities Press, 1987), p. 22.

16. "My Way to Hasidism," in ibid., pp. 61f. Hans Kohn suggests that the principle governing Buber's rendition of Hasidic tales may have been inspired by his friend Gustav Landauer's first modern German edition of Meister Eckhart's mystical writings, *Meister Eckharts Mystische Schriften, in unsere Sprache uebertragen von Gustav Landauer* (Berlin: Karl Schnmabel Verlag, 1903). See Kohn, *Martin Buber. Sein Werk und seine Zeit, ein Beitrag zur Geistesgeschichte Mitteleuropas, 1880–1930*, 2nd ed. (Cologne: Joseph Melzer Verlag, 1961), p. 30. See Landauer's explanation of his rendition of Eckhart's teachings, cited in *Meister Eckharts Mystische Schriften*, p. 239. Both Landauer's and Buber's concepts of re-telling (*Nacherzaehlung*) would seem to be influenced by Wilhelm Dilthey. On Buber's indebtedness to Dilthey, see *Ecstatic Confessions, Collected and Introduced by Martin*

*Buber*, trans. Esther Cameron, with introduction by P. Mendes-Flohr (San Francisco: Harper & Row, 1985), p. 16.

17. Cited in Hans Kohn, *Martin Buber*, p. 238.

18. *Ecstatic Confessions*, p. xxxi.

19. On Buber's relation to Dilthey, see Grete Schaeder, *The Hebrew Humanism of Martin Buber*, trans. N. J. Jacobs (Detroit: Wayne State University Press, 1973), pp. 41–46; also see Mendes-Flohr, *Von der Mystik zum Dialog*, ch. 2.

20. "The Imagination and the Poet" (1887), in Dilthey, *Poetry and Experience, Wilhelm Dilthey. Selected Works*, ed. R. A. Makkreel and F. Rodi (Princeton: Princeton University Press, 1985), p. 45.

21. *Truth and Method*, trans. from 2nd ed. by Garret Barden and John Cumming (New York: The Seabury Press, 1975), pp. xi, xxiii.

22. "Hasidism and Modern Man," pp. 22–23.

23. *Georg Lukács. Selected Correspondence, 1902–1920*, ed. and trans. Judith Marcus and Zoltan Tar (New York: Columbia University Press, 1986), pp. 172f. On the basis of the original German, we have modified the translation.

24. Ibid., p. 176f.

25. Cf. Buber, *The Tales of the Hasidim*, trans. Olga Marx (New York: Schocken Books, 1968), 2 vols.

26. The problems faced by Buber and all students of Hasidic literature are discussed *in extenso* by Ze'ev Gries, "Hasidism: The Present State of Research and some Desirable Priorities." *Numen*, xxxiv (1987): 97–108 (Part 1).

27. Martin Buber Archive, varia 350, dalet 2 a/1. At first Buber added before the sentence cited, "The Baal Shem said:"—but he crossed this out and added as a preface, "Rabbi Nachman has transmitted to us this saying of his greatgrandfather: . . ." He also added the title "Die kleine Hand" (The Small Hand). In *The Tales of Rabbi Nachman*, he entitled the passage in which the citation from the Baal Shem is found, albeit in a conflated form, "Beholding the World." In his notes, Buber also recorded the original Hebrew and the full bibliographical details.

28. *The Tales of Rabbi Nachman*, p. 35.

29. Emunah Yaron, "From the Correspondence of S.Y.

Agnon and Martin Buber," *Iton* 77, No. 66–67 (July/August 1985), p. 27 (Hebrew).

30. These sayings have been published in German by Michael Brocke, "Martin Buber und Rabbi Nachman von Bratzlaw," in *Orientierung. Katholische Blaetter fuer weltanschauliche Information*, XL1X/.23 (30 June 1985), pp. 138–41. The sayings will also be included in the revised German edition of *Die Geschichten des Rabbi Nachman*, mit einem Nachtwort von Paul Mendes-Flohr und Ze'ev Gries (Heidelberg: Verlag Lambert Schneider, 1988).

Paul Mendes-Flohr and Ze'ev Gries

# RABBI NACHMAN
# AND
# JEWISH MYSTICISM

# JEWISH
# MYSTICISM

Rabbi Nachman of Bratzlav, who was born in 1772 and died in 1810, is perhaps the last Jewish mystic. He stands at the end of an unbroken tradition whose beginning we do not know.

For a long time men sought to deny this tradition; today it can no longer be doubted. It has been proved that it was nourished by Persian, then by late-Greek, then even by Albigensian sources; but it preserved the power of its own stream, receiving all influx without being mastered by it. We can, of course, no longer look on it as its old masters and disciples did: as "Kabbala," that is, as transmission of the teaching from mouth to ear and again from mouth to ear in such a way that each generation receives it, yet each with a broader and richer interpretation until at the end of time the entire truth has been made known. Yet we must recognize its unity, its individuality, and, at the same time, the many limitations out of which it developed. Jewish mysticism may appear quite disproportionate, often confused, at times trivial when we compare it with Meister Eckhart, with Plotinus, with Lao-tzu; still it remains the marvelous bloom of an ancient tree. Its color strikes us as almost all too dazzling, its fragrance strikes us as almost all too luxuriant; yet it is one of the great manifestations of ecstatic wisdom.

The tendency toward mysticism is native to the Jews from antiquity, and its expressions are not to be understood, as usually happens, as a temporary conscious reaction against the dominance of the rule of the intellect. It is a significant peculiarity of the Jew, which hardly seems to have changed in thousands of years, that with him one extreme quickly and powerfully enkindles another. Thus it happened that in the midst of an unspeakably circumscribed existence, indeed out of its very limitations, there suddenly broke forth the limitless which now governed the soul that surrendered itself to it.

If, then, the strength of Jewish mysticism arose from an original characteristic of the people that produced it, so the later destiny of this people has also left its imprint on it. The wandering and martyrdom of the Jews have again and again transposed their souls into that vibration of despair out of which, at times, the lightning flash of ecstasy breaks forth. But at the same time they have hindered them from attaining the pure expression of ecstasy. They have led them to confuse the necessary, the actually experienced, with the superfluous, the borrowed, and, through the feeling that their pain was too great for them to express what was their own, to become loquacious about the alien. Thus arose works like the "Zohar," the "Book of Splendor." In the midst of gross speculations, glimpses of silent depths of the soul again and again light up.

In the time of the Talmud the mystical teaching was still a mystery that one might entrust only to a "master of the arts and one versed in the whispers." Only later did the teaching reach beyond the sphere of personal transmission. The oldest writing that has been preserved to us, the Pythagorizing "Book of Creation," seems to have arisen between the seventh and the ninth century, and the "Zohar" stems—at least in its present form—from the end of the thirteenth; between the two lies the time of the real unfolding of the Kabbala. But for a long while yet those who occupied themselves with the Kabbala remained limited to a narrow circle, even though this circle extended from France, Spain, Italy, and Germany to

Egypt and Palestine. During this whole period the teaching itself remains alien to life; it is theory in the Neoplatonic sense, vision of God, and desires nothing of the reality of human existence. It does not demand that one live it, it has no contact with action. The realm of choice that meant everything to Hasidism, the later Jewish mysticism, is not immediately alive for it. It is extra-human, touching the reality of the soul only in the contemplation of ecstasy.

Only in the late ages of this epoch did new powers manifest themselves. The expulsion of the Jews from Spain gave the Kabbala its great Messianic drive. The only energetic attempt of the Diaspora to establish in exile a culture-creating community and a homeland in spirit, had ended in ruins and despair. The old abyss again opened up, and out of it again ascended, as always, the old dream of redemption, imperative as never before since the days of the Romans. The longing burned: the absolute *must* become reality. The Kabbala could not shut its eyes to it. It called the kingdom of God on earth "the world of restoration." It took the fervor of the people into itself.

The new era of Jewish mysticism which began around the middle of the sixteenth century and which proclaimed the ecstatic act of the individual as a co-working with God to achieve redemption, was in-

augurated by Isaac Luria. In his ideas about the
emanation of the world out of God and the demiurgic
intermediary power he was almost entirely dependent
on the older Kabbala; but in his presentation of the
direct influence on God and the redeeming power of
the human soul that purifies and perfects itself, he
gives the old wisdom a new shape and a new consequence.

Already in the Talmud it says that the Messiah will
come when all souls have entered into corporeal life.
The Kabbalists of the Middle Ages believed they
could tell whether the soul of a man who stood before them had descended into him from the world of
the unborn or was temporarily staying with him in
the midst of its wanderings. The Zohar and the later
Kabbala developed the teaching that received its final
form from Isaac Luria. According to this teaching,
there are two forms of metempsychosis: the revolution
or wandering, *gilgul,* and the superabundance or im-
pregnation, *ibbur. Gilgul* is the entrance into a man,
in the moment of his conception or birth, of a soul that
is on the journey. But a man who is already endowed
with a soul can also, in a certain moment of his life,
receive one or more souls that unite themselves with
his own if they are related to it, that is, have arisen
out of the same radiation of the primordial man. The

7

soul of a dead man joins itself with that of a living man in order to be able to complete an unfinished work that it had to leave when it died. A higher, more detached spirit descends in complete fullness of light or in individual rays to an imperfect one to dwell with him and help him to completion. Or two uncompleted souls unite in order to supplement and purify each other. If weakness and helplessness overcomes one of these souls, then the other becomes its mother, bears it in its womb and nourishes it with its own being. By all these means the souls are purified of the primal darkening and the world redeemed from the original confusion. Only when this is done, when all the journeys are completed, then only does time shatter and the Kingdom of God begin. Last of all, the soul of the Messiah descends into life. Through him the uplifting of the world to God takes place.

Luria's special contribution is that he wanted to found this world process on the action of some men. He proclaimed an unconditional conduct of life for those who dedicated themselves to redemption; in ritual immersion baths and night watches, in ecstatic contemplation and unconditional love for all, they would purify the souls in a storm and call down the Messianic kingdom.

The basic feeling of which this teaching was the

ideal utterance found its elemental expression almost a hundred years later in the great Messianic movement that bears the name of Sabbatai Zvi. It was an eruption of the unknown powers of the people and a revelation of the hidden reality of the folk-soul. The seemingly immediate values, life and possessions, had suddenly become flat and worthless, and the people were now inclined to abandon the latter as a superfluous instrument and to hold the former only with a light hand, as a garment that slips away from the runner and that, if it hinders him too much, he can let slip by opening his fingers, in order to hurry, naked and free, to the goal. The race, supposed to be ruled by reason, became inflamed with ardor for the message.

This movement, too, collapsed, more pitifully than any of the earlier ones. And now Messianism once again intensifies itself. The real age of mortification begins. The belief in being able to compel the upper world through mystical exercises penetrates ever more deeply into the people. About the year 1700 is consummated that ascetic march of the Fifteen Hundred that ended in death and misery. But single individuals also prepare themselves in unsparing renunciation. In Poland, in particular, there ripens in many the will to atone for themselves and the world. Since no individual chastisement is enough for them, many of them set out upon the wandering—"in the exile," as they call it—nowhere accepting food or drink, and wandering thus, borne by their will, until their life is extinguished along with their strength and they drop dead in a strange place among strangers.

These martyrs of the will are the forerunners of Hasidism, the last and highest development of Jewish mysticism. Arising about the middle of the eighteenth century, Hasidism at once continued and counteracted the Kabbala. Hasidism is the Kabbala become ethos. But the life that it teaches is not asceticism but joy in God. The word Hasid designates a "pious man," but it is a world-piety that is meant here. Hasidism is no pietism. It dispenses with all sentimentality and emotional display. It brings the transcendent over into the immanent and lets the transcendent rule in it and form it, as the soul forms the body. Its core is a highly realistic guidance to ecstasy as to the summit of existence. But ecstasy is not here, as, say, in German mysticism, the soul's *"Entwerden,"* but its unfolding; it is not the self-restraining and self-renouncing, but the self-fulfilling soul which flows into the Absolute. In asceticism the spiritual being, the *neshama,* shrinks, sleeps, becomes empty and bewildered; only in joy can it awaken and fulfill itself until, free from all lack, it matures to the divine.

Again it was Poland that proved itself creative and above all the steppe-like plains of the Ukraine. Poland had a solid Jewish community, strengthened in itself by the alien, disdainful environment, and here for the first time since the Spanish flowering there unfolded a life of activity and values of its own, an indigent and frail, yet independent culture. If, then, the presuppositions for spiritual activity were thus given in general, still a mystical teaching could shoot up only on the soil of the Ukraine. Here, since the Cossack massacres of the Jews under Chmielnicki, there prevailed a condition of deepest insecurity and despair similar to that which once had rejuvenated the Kabbala after the expulsion from Spain. Moreover, the Jew was here mostly a villager, limited in his knowledge, but original in faith and strong in his dream of God.

The founder of Hasidism was Israel from Mesbisz (Miedjyborz), called the "Baal-Shem-Tov," that is, "Master of the Good Name," a designation that unites two things, the powerful, efficacious knowledge of the name of God, as the earlier wonder-working "Baale-Shem" were described, and the possession of a "good name" in the human sense of being trusted by the people. Around him and his disciples a colorful

**11**

and intimate legend wove itself. He was a simple, genuine man, inexhaustible in fervor and guiding power.

The teaching of the Baal-Shem is preserved for us very incompletely. He himself did not write it down, and even orally, as he once said, he communicated only what caused him, like an all-too-full vessel, to overflow. Among his disciples he seems to have found none worthy to receive the whole of his thought; a prayer by him has been handed down to us: "Lord, it is known and manifest to you how much rests in me of understanding and power, and there is no man to whom I could reveal it." But of what he did teach, much seems to have been most inadequately written down, often entirely distorted. On looking once through one such transcript, he is said to have cried out, "There is not *one* word here that I have spoken."

Nonetheless, the real sense of his teaching is unmistakable.

God, so the Baal-Shem teaches, is in each thing as its primal essence. He can only be apprehended by the innermost strength of the soul. If this strength is liberated, then it is given to man at each place and at each time to receive the divine. Each action which is dedicated in itself, though it appear ever so lowly and meaningless to those who see it from the outside, is the way to the heart of the world. In all things, even in those that appear completely dead, there dwell sparks of life that fall into the souls that are ready. What we call evil is no essence, but a lack. It is "God's exile," the lowest rung of the good, the throne of the good. It is—in the language of the old Kabbala—the "shell" that surrounds and disguises the essence of things.

There is nothing that is evil and unworthy of love. Even the urges of man are not evil: "the greater a man, the greater his urge."

The pure and holy man makes out of his urge "a chariot for God"; he delivers it from all shells and allows his soul to complete itself therein. Man must feel his urges in their depths and take possession of them. "He shall learn to know pride and not be proud, know anger and not become angry. And so it is with all qualities. Man shall become whole in all qualities. . . . The wise man may glance at whatever place he will and not stray beyond his four ells." The fate of man is only the expression of his soul: he whose thoughts roam about among unclean things finds the unclean in his life; he who submerges himself in the holy, experiences salvation. The thought of man is his being: he who thinks of the upper world is in it.

All outward teaching is only an ascent to the inward; the final aim of the individual is to become himself a teaching. In reality, the upper world is not an outward but an inward one; it is "the world of thought."

If, then, the life of man is open to the absolute in every situation and in each activity, man should also live his life in devotion. Each morning is a new summons. "He arises in eagerness from his sleep, for he is sanctified and has become another man and is worthy to create, and imitates God by forming his world." Man finds God on all ways, and all ways are full of unification. But the purest and most perfect is the way of prayer. When a man prays in the fire of his being, God Himself speaks the innermost word in his breast. This is the event; the external word is only its garment. "As the smoke ascends from burning wood, but the heavy part cleaves to the ground and becomes ashes, so from prayer only the will and the fervor ascend, but the external words crumble to ashes." The higher the fervor, the more powerful the strength of intention—kavana—so much the deeper is the transformation. "It is a great grace of God that man remains alive after prayer, for by nature he ought to die since he has buried his strength and entered into his prayer for the sake of the kavana that he fosters. . . . He thinks before praying that he is ready to die for the sake of the *kavana*." Prayer shall not take place in pain and repentance, however, but in great joy. Joy alone is true service of God.

The teachings of the Baal-Shem soon found access to the people, who were not equal to its idea yet eagerly welcomed its feeling for God. The piety of this people was inclined from of old to mystical immediacy; it received the new message as an exalted expression of itself. The proclamation of joy in God, after a thousand years of a dominance of law that was poor in joy and hostile to it, acted like a liberation. In addition, the people up till then had acknowledged above them an aristocracy of Talmud scholars, alienated from life, yet never contested. Now the people, by a single blow, were liberated from this aristocracy and established in their own value. Now it was said to them that it is not knowledge that determines the quality of a man, but the purity and devotion of his soul, that is, his nearness to God. The new teaching came like a revelation of what before then one had not dared to hope for. It was received like a revelation.

Naturally, the orthodox declared war on the new heresy and conducted it by all means—excommunication, closing of synagogues and burning of books, imprisonment and public mistreatment of the leaders—

not even shrinking from denunciation to the government. Nonetheless, the outcome of the battle could not here be in doubt: religious rigidity could not withstand the religious renewal. A more dangerous opponent to this renewal arose in the Haskala, the Jewish movement of enlightenment which, in the name of knowledge, of civilization, and of Europe, came forward against "superstition." But it too, which wanted to negate the people's longing for God, would not have been able to wrest a foot of ground from the movement which satisfied this longing if there had not commenced in Hasidism itself a decomposition that led to the decline that has continued since then.

The first cause of this decline lay in the fact that Hasidism demanded from the people a spiritual intensity and collectedness that they did not possess. It offered them fulfillment, but at a price they could not pay. It indicated as the bridge to God a purity and clarity of vision, a tension and concentration of the spiritual life of which only a few are ever capable; yet it spoke to the many. And so there arose out of the spiritual need of the people an institution of mediators who were called *zaddikim*, that is, righteous. The theory of the mediator who lives in both worlds and is the connecting link between them, through whom prayers are born above and blessing brought below, unfolded ever more exuberantly and finally overran all other teaching. The zaddik made the Hasidic community richer in security of God, but poorer in the one thing of value—one's own seeking. To this was added the growing external abuses. At first, only the really worthy, most of them disciples and disciples of disciples of the Baal-Shem, became zaddikim. But because the zaddik received from his community an ample livelihood in order to be able to devote to it the whole of his service, soon lesser men crowded to the benefice, and because they could offer nothing else, acquired a claim through all kinds of wonder-working. In many places an imposture prevailed which repulsed the purer, degraded the more definite, and attracted the most confused crowd of people.

17

# RABBI NACHMAN
## OF BRATZLAV

The period of the beginning degeneration of Hasidism is a profoundly tragic one. There arose men who saw the decline come and wanted to halt it, but were not able to. Among those who, apart from the belief in the zaddik, sought to restore the pure thought of the teaching, was the great thinker called Shneor Zalman who elaborated the panentheistic element of the Hasidic idea into a system of monumental strength and unity. But he could not become sufficiently popular actually to check the deterioration. Alongside him and his emulators, however, there were also those who certainly recognized the perversion of the institution of the zaddik, yet wanted not to annihilate it but to heal it, demanding in the place of the empty and deceitful wonder-worker, the dedicated mediator living in devotion. These latter ran aground on the smallness of men. Like the prophets of Israel, so too these, their late sons, were no reformers but revolutionaries; they demanded not the better, but the absolute; they wanted not to educate, but to redeem.

Among them the greatest and most tragic is Rabbi Nachman ben Ssimha, who is called Rabbi Nachman of Bratzlav after the chief place of his activity. He proposed "to restore to the crown its old splendor." The wrath against the defilers of the Temple burned in him. "The evil spirit," he used to say, "finds it hard to trouble himself with the whole world in order to divert it from the true way; therefore, he sets a zaddik here and a zaddik there." Rabbi Nachman did not want "to be a leader like the leaders to whom the pious journey and do not know why they journey." He had a great dream of the zaddik who is "the soul of the people." To this dream he sacrificed all the welfare and all the hope of his personal life. In it he placed all his striving and all his powers. And for its sake he was poor and surrounded by enemies until the end. Through it, while yet young and before the completion of his task, he found his death. And because he lived so wholly in his dream, he disdained to write down his teaching so that, as of the first master of Hasidism so of the last, we possess no genuine and direct message. Out of the fragmentary report of his disciples, who noted down his speeches, talks, and narratives and described his life, we are able to construct for ourselves—after many deletions, collations, and supplements—only an incomplete image of his reality.

Rabbi Nachman was a great-grandchild of the Baal-Shem and was born in Mesbisz, the city of the Baal-Shem. His childhood is described as a strenuous seeking and contending. He did not heed the commandment to serve in joy, tormented himself, fasted, and avoided rest in order to partake of the vision. The strong tradition of ecstatic life in his family dominated the boy, and he could not endure the slow, heavy course of existence, organized by day and night, determined by the affairs of the hours. The community's service of God also brought him no relief. So he ran at night to some place empty of men and spoke to God in the language of the people, in that tenderly blunt, melancholy, and bitter idiom that the European calls jargon. But God did not answer him. Then it seemed to him as if God "paid no attention to him, indeed removed him from service, He did not want him at all," and the storm of despair overwhelmed him and shook him until in the deepest despair ecstasy was kindled and the boy felt the first shudder of rapture.

Once in his later years he himself told of such an experience. He had wanted to receive the Sabbath in

**21**

great dedication, had gone around midnight into the ritual bath and had plunged into the water, his soul ready for sanctification. Then he had returned to the house and put on his Sabbath clothes. He now went into the prayer house and wandered up and down in the lonely, dark rooms, all of his powers strained in the will to receive the higher soul which descends into men on the Sabbath. He bound all his senses into one and concentrated all the force of his spirit in order to behold something, for now the revelation *must* come to him. But he saw nothing. He wanted to expire in order to behold, but he saw nothing. Meanwhile the first worshipers came into the prayer house, took their places and began to intone Canticles without noticing the boy. Then he crept to a prayer stand, laid himself under the stand and leaned his head on its foot, and the tears came to him. Thus he wept very quietly, without pausing and without looking up, hour after hour, until his eyes were swollen from much weeping and the evening began. Then he opened his eyes, which the weeping had closed, and the candle flames of the prayer house beat against him like a great light, and his soul grew peaceful in the light.

Thus he often suffered for God and would not desist. But he kept his life and his will hidden from the people. He employed all kinds of stratagems in order to conceal his fasting and when he went on the streets, he practiced every sort of childishness, prank, and trick until it did not occur to anyone that the boy yearned for the service of God. But the yoke of service was not always easy for him: he had a joyous, strong disposition and a fresh sense for the beauty of the world. Only later did he succeed in basing his devotion on just this disposition and serving God in joy. But at that time the world seemed to him something external that hindered him from coming to God. In order to persist in his struggling, he thought every morning that only this one day was still left to him; and at night he ran to the grave of his great-grandfather so that the Baal-Shem might help him. Thus flowed away the years of his childhood.

At fourteen, in accordance with the custom of the Jews of that time, he was married and settled in the village where his father-in-law dwelt. Here for the first time he came near to nature, and it gripped him in his innermost heart. After a childhood lived in the confinement of the city, the Jew who emerged into the free country was seized by a nameless power unknown to the non-Jew. A thousand-year heritage of strangeness to nature had held his soul in bonds. And now, as in a magical realm, instead of the pale-yellow walls of the streets, forest greenery and forest blooms

**23**

surrounded him; the walls of his spiritual ghetto tum-
bled down at once upon contact with the power of
growing things.

Seldom, indeed, has this experience announced itself
in so penetrating a manner as with Nachman. The
tendency toward asceticism withdraws from him, the
inner conflict ends, he no longer needs to trouble himself about revelation; easy and glad, he finds his God
in all things. The boat on which he journeys out on
the stream—unskilled with the rudder but full of confidence—leads him to God, whose voice he hears in
the reeds; and the horse that bears him into the forest
—obeying him, to his astonishment—brings him nearer
to God, who looks at him from all the trees and with
whom each plant is on intimate terms. In all the mountain slopes and in all the small hidden valleys of the
environs he is at home, and each is to him another way
to come to God.

At that time there took shape in him the teaching
of the service in nature that he later proclaimed, ever
again and with ever new praises, to his disciples.
"When man becomes worthy," he said to them, "to
hear the songs of the plants, how each plant speaks its
song to God, how beautiful and sweet it is to hear
their singing! And, therefore, it is good indeed to
serve God in their midst in solitary wandering over

24

the fields between the growing things and to pour
out one's speech before God in truthfulness. All the
speech of the fields enters then into your own and
intensifies its strength. With every breath you drink
in the air of paradise, and when you return home, the
world is renewed in your eyes." The ardent love for
all that is living and growing was strong in him. When
once, in the last period of his life, he slept in a house
that was built out of young trees, he dreamed that he
lay in the midst of the dead. In the morning he complained to the owner and accused him. "For when one
cuts down a tree before its time, it is as if one had
murdered a soul."

From the village he came into a small town where
he began to instruct one person and another in the
Hasidic teaching and to become known among the
pious. He was accosted by the temptation to be like
the zaddikim of the time and to live in fame, profit,
and idleness, but he withstood it. The decline of
Hasidism oppressed his soul. He missed the progress
of the teaching; the torch that should go from hand
to hand was extinguished in sluggish fingers. Thus in
Nachman's heart out of the sadness rose the will to
renew the tradition and "to make out of it a thing that
will endure forever." What the Kabbala had never
been, it should now become: the teaching should go

from mouth to ear and again from mouth to ear, steadily expanding itself out of the compass of the still unborn words, borne by an incessantly self-restoring band of messengers, awakening the spirit in each generation, rejuvenating the world, "turning the wilderness of the hearts into a dwelling-place for God."

But he knew that he could not draw the strength for such teaching out of books, but only out of actual life with men. So he drew close to the people, took all their suffering and their longing into himself, wished to grow entirely together with them. "In the beginning," he later related, "I wished of God that I might suffer the pain and need of Israel. But now, when one person tells me his pain, I feel the pain more than he does. For he can think other thoughts and forget the pain, but not I." Thus he lived with the people, as the Baal-Shem and his disciples had done, and found in them his consecration.

But before he began to teach to many, he wished to receive the blessing of the Holy Land, which is the heart of the world. He wished to behold the graves of Simeon ben Johai and Isaac Luria and to hear the voices which hover over the resting places of the prophets. The Baal-Shem had not been able to go to Palestine; signs and manifestations, so the legend tells, had bid him return shortly before the goal was reached. Rabbi Nachman found the journey very difficult. He was poor and had no other alternative than to give up his household, place his wife and children in service or in the merciful care of strangers, and sell all the furniture of his dwelling in order to raise the cost of the trip. Still the pious of the neighborhood, who heard of his resolve, facilitated its execution by collecting a sum of gold and presenting it to him. His relatives pleaded with him to desist from the journey, but he always said only, "My greater part is already there." Thus in 1798, with one of the pious who was willing to serve him, he began the trip. From this journey on, Nachman dated his real life. "All that I knew before *Erez Israel* (the land of Israel) is nothing at all," he used to say and forbade the preservation in writing of any of his earlier teachings. Palestine became for him a vision that did not leave him. "My place," he said, "is only Erez Israel, and wherever I travel, I travel to Erez Israel." And even in the last days of his sickness and weariness he affirmed, "I live only by the fact that I was in Erez Israel."

Shortly after his return, he settled in Bratzlav. But already before he came there, some zaddikim who hated him on account of his views had kindled a furious fight against him that continued until the end of his life and engendered wild hostilities; even after his death the communities of the others made war upon his own and would know no peace. He himself was not surprised at the strife. "How should they not contend with us?" he often said. "We do not belong at all to the present world, and therefore the world cannot tolerate us." It did not occur to him to retaliate for their enmity. "The whole world is full of strife, every country and every city and every house. But he who accepts in his heart the reality that a man dies every day, for every day he must deliver to death a piece of himself, how shall he still be able to pass his days in strife?" He never wearied of finding good in his adversaries and justifying them. "Am I then he whom they hate?" he asks. "They have carved out a man for themselves and contend with him." And he repeated the parable of the Baal-Shem: "Once some musicians stood and played, and a great group moved in dance in accordance with the voices of the music. Then a deaf man came there who knew nothing of dancing and music and thought in his heart, 'How foolish these men are: some beat with their fingers on all kinds of implements, and others turn themselves this way and that.'" Thus Rabbi Nachman justified his enemies. Indeed, he regarded their rage as a blessing: "All words of slander and all fury of enmity against the genuine and the silent are like stones that are thrown against him, and out of them he builds his house."

In Bratzlav he began to teach many and gathered many about him. Teaching was for him a mystery and his whole deed full of mystery. Communication for him was not an ordinary event about which one does not need to reflect because it is so familiar and well known. Rather it was rare and wonderful, like something newly created. One feels his astonishment at the way of words when he says, "The word moves a bit of air, and this the next, until it reaches the man who receives the word of his friend and receives his soul therein and is therein awakened." The word that only reports a sense impression hastily and unsatisfactorily he despises, and the pious "who immediately announce what they see and cannot hold it in" he values less than those "whose root is in the fullness and who can keep to themselves what they see." But the word that ascends out of the ground of the soul is to him an exalted thing whose living activity is no longer the work of the soul but the soul itself. He speaks no word of instruction that has not passed through much suffering; each is "washed in tears." The word forms itself late in him; the teaching is with him at first an event and only then becomes a thought, that is, a word. "I have in me," he said, "teachings without clothes, and it is very hard for me until they clothe themselves." There is always in him a dread of the word, which compresses his throat, and before he speaks the first word of a teaching, it seems to him as if his soul must expire.

Only the effect of his word assuages him. He contemplates it and wonders over it: "At times my words enter like a silence into the hearers and rest in them and work later, like slow medicines; at times my words do not at first work at all in the man to whom I say them, but when he then says them to another, they come back to him and enter into his heart in great depth and do their work in perfection." This second basic relation, the receiving of one's own word, is characteristic of the Jew with his motor tendency, and Rabbi Nachman also seems to have experienced it in himself. He represented it once in the image of the reflection of light: "When one speaks to one's fellow, there arises a simple light and a returning light. But it occasionally happens that the former is present without the latter; then his fellow often does not receive from him, but he receives awakening from his fellow when through the impact of the words that proceed from his mouth the light returns to him and is awakened."

The decisive thing for Nachman, in accordance

with his interpretation of the word, is not, of course, the effect on the speaker, but on the hearer. This effect reaches its climax in the fact that the relationship changes and the hearer becomes a speaker, so that, in fact, *he* speaks the final word. The soul of the disciple shall be summoned in its depths so that out of it, and not out of the soul of the master, the word will be born that proclaims the highest meaning of the teaching, and thus the conversation is fulfilled in itself. "When I begin to talk with someone, I want to hear the highest words from *him*."

Rabbi Nachman was five years in Bratzlav when he fell ill with consumption, probably under the influence of the fights and persecutions, by which he remained untouched in his soul but which he could not withstand in his body. It was soon clear to him that he must die, but his own death was never a subject of anxiety to him and even not an important event at all. "To him who attains the true knowledge, the knowledge of God, there is no separation between life and death, for he cleaves to God and embraces Him and lives the eternal life like Him." He received death rather as an ascent to a new stage of great wandering, to a more perfect form of total life; and because he believed that in this human body he could attain to no higher rung of perfection than that which he had reached, he longed for death and for the dark threshold. "I would already gladly take off the little shirt," he said to his disciples in his last year, "for I cannot bear to remain standing on one rung."

When he recognized that death was approaching him, he no longer wanted to remain in Bratzlav where he had taught and worked, but decided to move to Uman in order to die and be buried there. In 1768, a few years before his birth, the bands of the Haidamaks had penetrated into Uman; and after its fortress, defended in common by Jews and Poles, had fallen to them through artifice and treachery, they had murdered the entire Jewish population and thrown their corpses in piles on the city wall. It was Rabbi Nachman's belief, a result of the doctrine of the soul that he took over from Luria and further developed, that of the many thousands who had been slaughtered in Uman before their time, a great band of souls were bound to the place of their death and could not ascend until a soul came to them with the power to lift them. He felt in himself the summons to redeem the waiting ones, and he wanted, therefore, to die in their place and to have his grave next to theirs that the work might be accomplished over their graves. When he came to Uman, he dwelt in a house whose window looked out on the cemetery, "the house of life," as the

Jews call it; there he often stood in the window and looked down joyfully on the graveyard. Sometimes sadness overtook him, but not about dying, rather about the work of his life that did not bear the fruit that he had dreamed. He pondered whether he would not have done better to have cast off the world and to have chosen for himself a secluded place in order to sit there alone so that the yoke of the world would not be on him. If only he had not taken up the leading of men, he thought, perhaps he would have reached his perfection and done his true deed. The teaching and educating that he had so extolled appeared to him in such moments as a wrong, almost as a sin. For the essence of service in each thing is that man shall be left to his own choice. It also seemed to him there that he had accomplished little, and he perceived how hard it is to make a man free. It is more difficult to help with service and to uplift *one* righteous man, so long as he is still in the body, than to help and uplift a thousand thousands of evil ones who are already in the spirit, that is, to redeem their souls; for with a *master of choice* it is exceedingly difficult to effect something.

But in his last days all care and distress fell away from him. He prepared himself. "See," he once said, "a very great and lofty mountain comes toward us.

But I do not know: Are we going to the mountain, or is the mountain coming to us?" Thus he died in peace. A disciple wrote, "The countenance of the dead man was like the countenance of the living when he walked up and down in his studio and thought."

Rabbi Nachman did not accomplish his task. He had become the zaddik whom he meant, "the soul of the people"; but the people had not become his. He had not been able to halt the decline of the teaching. It was the flowering of the soul of the exile; but it also withered in exile. The Jews were not strong enough and pure enough to preserve it. It is not given to us to know whether a resurrection will be granted it. But the inner destiny of Judaism seems to me to depend on whether—no matter if in this shape or another—its pathos will again become deed.

# SAYINGS
# OF RABBI NACHMAN

*The World*

The world is like a revolving die, and everything turns over, and man changes to angel and angel to man, and the head to the foot and the foot to the head. So all things turn over and revolve and are changed, this into that and that into this, what is above to what is beneath and what is beneath to what is above. For in the root all is one, and in the transformation and return of things redemption is enclosed.

*Beholding the World*

As the hand held before the eye conceals the greatest mountain, so the little earthly life hides from the glance the enormous lights and mysteries of which the world is full, and he who can draw it away from before his eyes, as one draws away a hand, beholds the great shining of the inner worlds.

## God and Man

All the troubles of man proceed from himself. For the light of God continually pours over him, but man, through his all too physical life, makes himself a shadow so that the light of God cannot reach him.

## Faith

Faith is an immensely strong thing, and through faith and simplicity, without any subtleties, one becomes worthy of attaining the rung of grace, which is even higher than that of holy wisdom: abundant and powerful grace of God is given to him in holy silence until he can no longer endure the power of the silence and cries aloud out of the fullness of his soul.

## Prayer

Let everyone cry out to God and lift up his heart to Him, as if he were hanging by a hair and a tempest were raging to the very heart of heaven so that he did not know what to do, and he had almost no more time left to cry out. And in truth there is no counsel and no refuge for him save to remain alone and to lift up his eyes and his heart to God and to cry out to Him. One should do this at all times, for a man is in great danger in the world.

36

### Two Languages

There are men who can utter words of prayer in truth so that the words shine like a jewel that shines of itself. And there are men whose words are only like a window that has no light of its own, but only shines forth out of the light that it admits.

### Within and Without

Man is afraid of things that cannot harm him, and he knows it, and he craves things that cannot be of help to him, and he knows it; but in truth the one thing man is afraid of is within himself, and the one thing he craves is within himself.

### Two Kinds of Human Spirit

There are two kinds of spirit, and they are like backward and forward. There is one spirit that man attains in the course of time. But there is another spirit that overwhelms man in great abundance, in great haste, swifter than a moment, for it is beyond time and for this spirit no time is needed.

### Thinking and Speaking

All thoughts of man are speaking movement, even when he does not know it.

*Truth and Dialectic*

Victory cannot tolerate the truth, and if one displays a true thing before your eyes, you reject it for the sake of victory. He, then, who wants the truth in himself drives away the spirit of victory, for only then is he ready to behold the truth.

*The Aim of the World*

The world was created only for the sake of the choice and the choosing one.

Man, the master of choice, should say: The whole world has been created only for my sake. Therefore, man shall take care at every time and in every place to redeem the world and fill its want.

*Joy*

Through joy the spirit becomes settled, but through sadness it goes into exile.

*Perfection*

One must perfect oneself to unity until one is perfected in creation as he was before creation, so that he is wholly one, entirely good, thoroughly holy, as before creation.

One must renew oneself every day in order to perfect oneself.

### The Evil Urge

The evil urge is like one who runs about among men, and his hand is closed and no one knows what is in it. And he goes up to each and asks, "What do you suppose I have in my hand?" And each imagines that just what he most desires is in that hand. And everybody runs after it. And then he opens his hand, and it is empty.

One can serve God with the evil urge if one directs his passion and his fervor of desiring to God. And without the evil urge there is no perfect service.

In the righteous the evil urge is transformed into a holy angel, a being of might and destiny.

### Ascent

No limits are set to the ascent of man, and to each the highest stands open. Here your choice alone decides.

### Judging Oneself

If a man does not judge himself, all things judge him, and all things become messengers of God.

## Will and Obstacle

There is no obstacle that one cannot overcome, for the obstacle is only there for the sake of the willing, and in reality there are no obstacles save in the spirit.

## Between Men

There are men who suffer terrible distress and they cannot tell anyone of it, and they go about full of suffering. But if one meets them with laughing countenance, he may cheer them with his joy. And it is no small thing to cheer a man.

## In Concealment

There are men who have no authority at all when they reveal themselves, but in concealment they rule the generation.

## The Kingdom of God

Those who do not walk in loneliness will be bewildered when the Messiah comes and they are called; but we shall be like a man who has been asleep and whose spirit is tranquil and composed.

## The Wandering of the Soul

God never does the same thing twice. When a soul returns, another spirit becomes its companion.

When a soul comes into the world, its deed begins to ascend out of the hidden worlds.

There are naked souls who cannot enter into bodies, and for them there is great compassion, more than for those that have lived. For these latter were in bodies and have procreated and produced; but the former cannot ascend, and also they cannot descend to clothe themselves with bodies. There are wanderings in the world that have not yet revealed themselves.

The righteous must be unsettled and transient because there are fugitive souls who only thereby can ascend. And if a righteous man resists and will not wander, he becomes unsettled and transient in his house.

There are stones, like souls, that are flung down on the streets. But once the new houses are built, then one will fit into them the holy stones.

# THE
# STORIES

In the last years of his life Rabbi Nachman told his
disciples many fables and tales. It was always some
outward occasion that brought him to narrating. Some
of these occasions have come down to us.

Once one of his disciples reported to him what he
had just heard about the war of the French that was
going on at that time. "And we were astonished by
the exalted position to which that one [Napoleon] had
been raised so that from a lowly man [literally, "servant"] he had become an emperor. And we spoke with
*him* about it. And he said, 'Who knows whose soul
is his, for it may be that it was exchanged. For in the
castle of transformations souls are at times exchanged.'
And at once he began to tell us the tale of the king's
son and the son of the maid who were exchanged."

Another time a precentor of a synagogue came to
him, and his clothes were torn. Then he said to him,

"Are you not then a master of prayer through whom the blessing is brought downward? And you should go in torn garments!" Then he told the story of the master of prayer.

Still another time a disciple had written to another that he should be joyful. When the master heard of the letter, he said, "What do you know, how one can be glad in the midst of sorrow? I will tell you how people have rejoiced in days past." And he began the story of the seven beggars, the last of the stories and the one he did not finish.

What stimulated Rabbi Nachman to narration was his feeling that his teachings "have no clothes." They ought to "awaken." He wanted to plant a mystical idea or a truth of life in the hearts of his disciples. But without his intending it, the narration took shape in his mouth, grew beyond its aim and blossomed upward until it was no longer teaching, but a fable or a legend. The tales have not lost thereby their symbolic character, but they have become stiller and more. inward.

Rabbi Nachman found an already existing tradition of Jewish folk tales and joined with it. But he is the first real storyteller among the Jews. All earlier tales were anonymous creation; here there is present, for the first time, the person—personal intention and personal formation.

The tales were written down from memory by his disciples, particularly by his favorite disciple, Nathan of Nemirov, who was his true apostle. Most of the tales (especially those not included in his collection) were recorded in a garbled and fragmentary manner. Nathan, to be sure, in order not to forget them, used to tell the individual tales to two others immediately after hearing them and only then go home to write them down. But he often seems to have waited longer than that, for of many things he himself admitted that he had forgotten them, of still others that he had not written them down "at their time." From the words of teaching ascribed to Rabbi Nachman one can tell which have been immediately recorded; they show the spirit and the language of the master. The tales, in contrast, are all obviously deformed. Rabbi Nachman did not possess a disciple equal to him who could have filled in, in the spirit of the narrator, the parts of the stories that were forgotten. He himself, moreover, probably glanced here and there at the records of his words of teaching, but never at those of the tales. As a result, what two early historians of Hasidism said of the notes of the disciples applies above all to the tales: "They wrote things that he had never said," asserts the one, and the other judges, "They assimilated the word that he had spoken to their own thoughts."

Thirteen of the stories were published in 1815, after the death of the master, in the Yiddish original with Hebrew translation. Of these, six are set down here.

# THE TALES
# OF
# RABBI NACHMAN

# THE RABBI
# AND HIS SON

There was once a rabbi who had dedicated his life to
the Torah, applied all his mind to investigating it, and
guarded the law with all his will so that it should be
observed in the community even in the smallest de-
tail. When a single son was born to him in his late
years, this seemed to him a reward and an assent of
God. It was as if, from above, a confirmation of his
way of life had been allotted him, and he vowed to
himself that all the days that remained to him he
would see to it that his son, like him, penetrated the
depths of the teaching and did not diverge a hair's
breadth from the demand of the law. That his son,
like him, should be an enemy of those enthusiasts
who dared to join their rambling dreams to the primal
and everlasting might of the Torah.

The son grew up and became great in the wisdom
of the holy books. He had a little room in his father's

**49**

house where he used to sit, collecting all his senses in order to absorb himself in the mysteries of the scriptures. But his soul could not persevere over the books, and his glance did not stay on the endless surfaces of rigid letters, but again and again flew out over the yellow billows of corn to the dark streak of the distant fir woods. His soul flew thither with his glance and lulled itself in the silent air like a young bird. Yet he ever anew forced his eye and heart back into the narrow prison, for he wanted to know, and the knowledge was certainly in the books. But even though he held his head bent with both hands over the pages covered with signs, his soul still did not allow itself to be imprisoned. If it could not nourish itself on the abundance outside the window, then it looked within itself, as into an unknown and mysterious landscape.

Nevertheless, he grew strong in the knowledge of the teaching, although it was not from the maze of signs before him that his wisdom streamed; it was as if it came from within himself. At the same time, there grew in him that strength of being that is named holiness. Wisdom and holiness unite, however, in that incomprehensible transformation called "the rung of the lesser light," which appears from time to time in a single human soul and departs with it. But like one who imagined himself ignorant, although within himself he embraced the world, the son of the rabbi supposed that for the sake of the truth he must investigate the writings still further. As soon as he approached the books, however, he felt himself abandoned in a boundless void. So he returned ever again into the world of his inner vision. But in it, too, he did not find satisfaction.

He could not speak of it, for if he attempted to, his words said something quite different from what filled his mind. But of all men, he associated only with the Hasidim, with those very enthusiasts who were so hated by his father. He felt that in their manner, as excessive as it appeared, there lived something of what went through his dreams. His father was angry at him, but he could not give up his association with them. When he was once together with two of them, two youths, he fortified his heart and struggled with the words until they obeyed him. He told the two youths how he languished for an unnamable.

They said to him, "There is one who can help you. That is the great zaddik who dwells a day's journey from here. For to him is given the power to liberate souls. When he goes through the ranks of men, divine blessing pours upon them out of his eyes. If he stretches his hand toward the oppressed, they breathe again. He wipes the signs of sorrow and distress from men's foreheads. He relaxes the spasm of hatred in men's hearts. To the dejected he shows the beauty of the world."

"Is he learned?" asked the youth. "We do not know whether he is learned," they answered, "for he never speaks of the things by which one judges whether a man is learned. But we do know this, that he acts upon the nearest and the farthest."

"Is he holy?" the youth asked further.

"We do not know whether he is holy," they said, "for he never holds himself aloof, and he does not shun contact with the sinful. But this we know well, that he does not leave anyone before he has taken from him the heaviest burden of his soul."

"But is it not so," he pursued, and he looked more within himself than at them, "that just this compassion is called 'the rung of the great light,' which appears at the rarest intervals in a single soul in order to shine forth to the thousands?"

Then the youths were silent and were struck by the vehemence of his words, which they had never before known in him.

From then on he was determined that he must betake himself to this zaddik. He communicated his intention to his father and asked his father to let him go. The father, however, regarded it as a great disgrace that his son desired to visit the foolish man of wonders and advanced all the reasons against it that were familiar to him. When the son persisted in his request, the father asked him to consider how little it became the learned son of a family of strict believers to seek his salvation with such a heretic, such a confused, vague, and muddleheaded thinker. So the father refused his son's request.

But soon everybody in the house became aware of how the life of the boy grew continually weaker through this unsatisfied longing. At another time when he again expressed his wish, the heart of the old man inclined to him, overcome by pity. He promised to comply with his son's desire and decided to lead his son to the zaddik himself; for the devotion to his only child was powerful in him, and he also hoped, in his secret heart, that his sagacity would succeed in making the stranger appear foolish and of no account. But in consenting, he said, "One thing, however, may be a sign to us that this journey is according to the will of heaven: that during the journey nothing happens that runs counter to the everyday course of events. But should something occur that hinders our steps, then this will be an indication that this way is not destined for you; in that case we shall return."

On the next day, father and son set out on the trip.

They had already gone a few hours' distance from their starting point, when the horse ran against a bridge and caused the carriage to fall. The two emerged uninjured, to be sure, but the old man ascribed to the accident a deeper significance and would not regard it otherwise than as representing a warning not to continue the journey. So they returned home.

From this hour on the youth was overtaken by such endless sadness that the father, compelled by his pleading, soon set out with him again on the trip. They already had a half day's journey behind them when suddenly the axle of the carriage broke and the rabbi, bewildered and anxious, since he could not explain the happening otherwise than as a higher decree, again gave up the journey and ordered their return home. And again the boy wasted away so that it gave the father too much pain to see it, and for a third time they began the journey.

This time the old man decided not to turn back and not to pay attention to any mishap unless something altogether out of the ordinary checked their path. So they traveled till evening, and only when darkness fell, did they seek out an inn. While they were resting in the parlor of the inn, they were joined by a traveling merchant with whom they soon entered into conversation. The rabbi had resolved not to mention his visit to the zaddik while talking, for it was firmly established in his mind that it was something to be ashamed of. So they spoke about many worldly things, and the old man was astonished at how well-versed and informed the stranger was in every sphere, and how cleverly and skillfully he knew how to guide the discussion. Soon the rabbi was like wax in his hands, and the strange guest learned whatever it pleased him to know. While they spoke of this and that, the merchant, entirely by chance, led the talk to the zaddikim and where particular ones were located. When the rabbi entered into the conversation with some curiosity, the merchant mentioned that not far from there lived a zaddik who had caused a great stir. At these words his gaze encompassed the youth, who up till now had sat there silent and absorbed, in a peculiarly flashing and penetrating manner. The youth took fright, as if a sharp pain had awakened him from sleep, and he now heard his father ask the stranger whether he knew this zaddik.

"Indeed I know him," responded the merchant with a scornful laugh.

"Then you undoubtedly know whether he is in fact that venerable and pious man that he is taken for?"

Then the stranger again laughed loudly and said,

"The zaddik, a pious and righteous man? Never have I met a worse worldling than he. With my own eyes I have seen his sinful urges, and I who came to him to seek help and support went from there disappointed and shocked."

The old man turned to his son and called out, "I suspected that it was as this upright man tells us. We shall return home. And now that you yourself have heard, you will free your heart from this madness.."

But when they had come back home, the son lay down and expired.

Boundless was the grief that this death brought to the old rabbi. But a few weeks afterwards, the dead boy appeared to the rabbi in a dream, flaming with wrath and terrifying to behold.

Trembling, the old man cried, "Why do I see you in such shape, my son?"

The apparition replied, "Set out on the way to that zaddik and you will learn why."

In the morning the rabbi remembered the occurrence, to be sure, but he believed that his senses had probably fooled him and that this was a dream just like any other. It came again, however, and it came a third time, and then the old man no longer dared to resist it and set out on the way to the zaddik.

Toward evening, when dusk and fatigue overcame

him, he entered an inn, and when he had sat for a while in the darkening parlor, he saw that it was the same parlor in which, a few weeks before, he had stayed with his now dead son. The thought shocked him out of his brooding; he looked about him and saw sitting opposite him the figure of the merchant whom he had also met at that time. On the rabbi's arrival, the room had been empty, and he had not noticed that anyone had entered. But his anguish was too insistent to allow him room for wondering. And he asked the stranger, "Are you not that merchant with whom I spoke here a short time ago?"

Then the latter broke into an unruly laugh and answered, "I am he, and what I wanted, I have succeeded in. Recall how you and your son wanted to go to the zaddik. First, your horse fell, and you turned back. Then the axle of your carriage broke, and you turned back again. And finally, you came and found me and listened to my words and turned back for the third time. And now, since I have killed your son, you may certainly go to the zaddik. For know that your son had the rung of the lesser light, but that zaddik had been given the rung of the great light, and if they had come together on earth, then the word would have been fulfilled and the Messiah would have appeared. But now, since I have killed your son, you may certainly go there!" After he had said this, he vanished, and the rabbi stared into empty space. The old man continued on his way, came to the zaddik, threw himself at his feet and cried, "Woe, woe for those who are so lost and who cannot be found again!"

# THE STEER
# AND THE RAM

In a distant land and at a distant time there reigned
a king. He isued a decree one day that all the Jews
who lived on the soil of his kingdom and under the
protection of his sword must receive baptism and
submit themselves to his creed, and that those who
refused must go from there and abandon home and
goods. There were many for whom their belief was
their only fatherland and possession: they fled abroad
in all directions. Others wanted to see the ripening
of the seed that they had sown and could not hide
their treasures in the mountains: they remained and
pretended to submit. Outwardly they practiced the
hated ceremonies of an alien faith; but behind secure
walls and fast bolts they adhered to the customs of
their old teaching and remained Jews as before, if
only secretly.

The king died, and after him his son ascended the

throne. This man held his vassals down with a harsh fist and subjugated foreign kingdoms by the force of his armies. The princes of lands which were heavily burdened by his harsh rule rebelled against him in secret and decided to murder him. Among them, however, was one of those Jews who only pretended to bear the fetters of an alien faith.

He said to himself, "For the sake of my possessions, to which my heart is attached, my creed avoids the sunlight. What will happen to these possessions if there is no king in the realm who can uphold the law and morality? Men will fall on one another like wild beasts, and the powerful will seize the possessions of the timid. It will profit me to go and warn the king."

He went and did so. The king listened to him and had the truth of his words checked, and they proved to be right. About the time when the conspirators wished to steal in, hidden bodyguards fell on them and brought them, subdued and fettered, before the king. He passed sentence on each according to the degree of his guilt.

But to his rescuer he spoke thus, "How may I reward you? I cannot offer you a princedom since you possess one already, and what jewels will outshine the abundance of your own? Let me know the wish that rests deepest within your heart, and be certain that it will be fulfilled."

The prince answered, "Let me be a Jew before all the world and practice my customs openly. Grant that I may put on prayer shawl and prayer straps without fear."

At this speech the soul of the king was embittered, for he hated the faith of the Jews. But compelled by his own word that he had given, he reluctantly acceded to the request.

The king passed away, and his son inherited the kingdom. From the fate of his father the knowledge had arisen in him that it would be good to lead the land in gentleness, and so he became a kind and mild ruler. At times he thought of the danger that had threatened his father's life, and then he was filled the whole day long with fear for the continuance of his family. One such time he had the astrologer called and commanded him to read in the signs of the heavens what was predestined for his family and what dangers threatened it. The magician found only two signs of evil portent—two animals, the steer and the ram; his family should beware of these, no other being could bring ruin to it. The king had the reading of fate entered in the book of memories, admonished his son to rule gently like him, and died soon after.

But the son who followed him to the throne was, like his forebears, of a rasher and more violent disposition. He afforded his armies no rest and preferred to settle affairs by force rather than by words. When he read, in the chronicle, of the two animals that threatened his house with ruin, it seemed to him quite simple to remove the danger: he forbade, under pain of death, the possession of steers and rams in the country, and from then on he knew no anxiety. He oppressed his subjects and laughed at their thoughts of revenge since he knew now that no conspiracy could harm his family line. But he loved to look through old books of magic in order to find hidden wisdom through which he could fortify and expand his might. He found there one day a passage in which the following was written:

"Seven planets shine upon the seven parts of the earth, and each part conceals its special metal that draws to it the rays of its star. He who sends messengers there, has the seven metals brought to him from the seven parts of the earth, has a metal giant cast out of them, and erects it upon a high mountain so that the light of the seven planets shines on it, can, through this figure, attract to himself the wisdom of the stars that revolve above the earth, acquire unheard-of power, and rule the world. For to every question that he directs to the giant, the answer of the stars will be made known to him through the illumination of the metals in secret signs."

The king had the statue erected on a high mountain, and when that was done, he secretly ascended the mountain in the dead of night and directed to the giant the question of how he could obtain the greatest power on earth. Then the metals began to shimmer, wonderful signs appeared, and he was able to decipher them. But their meaning was this: he must go back down to bring low the high and lift up the low; then he would rule all men. The king descended the mountain early the next morning, sought the wisest man of his land, disclosed to him the saying of the planets and asked him for an explanation of how he might act on it.

"From those of your subjects," replied the wise man, "who call dignities and offices their own without having earned them, who have possessions without having integrity, noble names without noble spirits, take what does not belong to them and what in their hands comes to mischief and give it to those who suffer evil without guilt and live in darkness in spite of their worth. Bear in mind also the Jews who through your forefathers were deprived of their homeland or had to deny their faith; open your country to them and permit them to acknowledge their faith freely."

The king was well pleased by the counsel to divest the rich and high, the mighty of his realm, of their possessions and honors; and it certainly seemed to be a way to power. But the direction to bestow possessions and power on the oppressed seemed to him strange and foolish; how easily violent adversaries might arise among them who, if they became strong, perhaps would find the circumstances favorable to repay him for the old wrongs! So he returned to his palace determined to alter the saying in accordance with his views. He had the books of the realm examined to find what investitures and honors, rights and titles, his forebears had conferred on the principal families; all of these he bid withdrawn in the name of the crown, and where resistance stirred, he commanded that it be broken by force.

But among the names that were recorded in the books as those of men who enjoyed preferences and distinctions, there was also found that of the Jew who had saved the life of the grandfather of the king. The king could not understand quite clearly of what the privilege of this man consisted, and so he sent for him and questioned him about it.

The old man said, "My reward is that I may confess myself a Jew before all the world."

"Then you have amply enjoyed the reward until today," cried the king. "I withdraw it from you, and you may live as before."

The Jew turned to go. In front of the palace he raised his hand and said to himself, "As sure as God may be moved to pity that from now on I must again wear prayer shawl and straps in the dark and behind closed doors, shall I curse you, cruel king, and your family."

After some time it came to pass that one night an oppressive dream descended on the king. He stood, so it seemed to him, on a broad plain. The night hid everything earthly in a cloak of darkness. But at an immense height an entirely clear heaven vaulted itself like a bell, and therein, sparkling like silver and resembling full-bodied figures, stood the twelve images of the zodiac. Two of them, the steer and the ram, seemed to him brighter than the others, and their rays appeared to shine directly on him. When he raised his glance to them, they began to laugh soundlessly so that his blood froze. This silent laughter became a horrible grinning. Then the king awakened. But fear clasped his heart with an iron clutch, and when he told the dream to the queen and his children, the horror seized them all, and there were none among them who had not thought of the old warning that stood in the chronicles: that the family was proof against all powers of ruin, and only by two animals, the steer and the ram, was its downfall threatened.

Runners were dispatched who brought back all the interpreters of dreams in the kingdom. But there were none among them who grasped the meaning of the vision, and the words of none were acceptable in the king's ears. He dismissed them with angry gestures and sent for the old wise man who had once explained to him the saying of the metal giant.

The king related the dream to him and said, "Save me, for fear has gripped my soul and threatens to suffocate it."

The wise man said, "I will lead you to where all the fear of the earth becomes naught. I know from the old books the one place alone in the world on which all three hundred and sixty-five journeys of the sun shine down. There, out of the core of the earth, there grows forth a tree of bronze that banishes all the distress of the outer surface and of the inner darkness. Follow me there with your family." The king agreed, and soon he and his whole household were prepared for the trip.

The wise man led the way for them, and they had

already gone far when they came to a place from which many paths branched out, and at the turning-point stood the powerful figure of an angel, who was the guardian over all the angels of wrath. For every earthly wrath, in conformity with the primordial will, creates a destroyer, an angel of wrath, and he who stood here at the parting of the ways was their ruler. He wore armor, blue lightning flashed from his eyes, and the sword in his hand blazed like a mighty flame. Trembling, the wanderers submitted to his direction as to where they had to go. He lifted his sword along one of the paths, and they walked on it.

But the wise man knew from the book of his ancestors that to each of the paths was imparted a meaning: one was straight and led to the place of eternal light; another was slippery, traversed by crawling worms, and led to a primordial slime; a third issued through frightful pits and grottoes into an abyss; but the last, full of scorching torments, was the way of fire. This was the way that they went at the bidding of the angel. Ominous dread seized the wise man. He had gone only a short stretch when he halted, for he already imagined that red-hot breezes scorched his throat, and he recalled that one of the ways led into spaceless fire and that four miles from its beginning the fire already consumes the traveler. When they had gone further a while, he perceived in the distance a red sea that flamed to heaven. Enclosed in its fiery flood, as in a bloody crystal, was a march of kings in the costumes of distant and unfamiliar peoples, and their ranks were led by ancient Jews who were wrapped in their prayer shawls and had wound round their foreheads and arms the holy straps. The wise man counseled the king and his family to turn back. But the king spurned his advice, for in his blindness he thought that, like those crowned figures, he could go unharmed through the fire. He had penetrated only a little way forward with his family when the bowels of flame greedily opened up and entombed them all. The wise man, however, had remained at his place and saw them go under. He turned around and retraced his steps. The angel had buried his sword in the earth. Fixed and silent, he let him walk past.

When the wise man had returned alone to the kingdom, he gathered all the people around him. He related to them the downfall which had been the lot of the king and his family. A great astonishment grew in the crowd, for all knew of the prophecy according to which the house of the king was promised destruction through a steer and a ram, but none could explain the outcome.

Then the old Jew who had had to practice his faith

in secret arose and said, "Through me he has been destroyed. The astrologers saw and knew not what they saw. But you may know this: from the hide of the steer the prayer straps are cut, and from the wool of the ram are spun the fringes that are attached to the prayer shawl. Therefore the steer and the ram derided him from among the stars. But those kings who were led uninjured through the fire were those in whose lands Jews live without harm and can wear prayer shawl and prayer straps in freedom."

# THE CLEVER MAN
## AND THE
## SIMPLE MAN

In a city in the east there lived two rich men who possessed many kinds of goods, long rows of houses, fields as far as the eye could reach, shining money in abundance, and valuables in which they could delight their hearts. Each of them had a son, and the two boys were very good to each other, played peaceably together, and also kept together in school. One was very clever, his understanding was sharp and bright, and nothing was so complex that he could not grasp it. The other was simple in nature and spirit, he could grasp what was simple and direct, no more and no less.

When the two boys had just outgrown their studies, it happened that the fathers became poor at the same time, and there remained to each one nothing save the house in which he dwelled. Then they spoke to their sons, "Take heed how you help yourselves

**71**

through the world. We cannot assist you since nothing more is our own save the roof over our heads."

The simple one, to whom the world appeared unconquerable, began to acquire a craft with a poor cobbler. But the clever one determined to conquer the world, turned his back on his home, and traveled to foreign places.

As he went along the highway, he came on a great wagon on which bundles of wares were piled and which the four horses drew with great difficulty. Alongside the wagon strode the merchant with his servants. When the clever one caught sight of them, he greeted them and joined them. They fell into talk and he learned that the merchant was from Warsaw and on his way home still had to take care of a great deal of business. When he asked him whether he still needed a handy servant and offered himself, the merchant was at once ready to try him out, for he had quickly recognized that he had before him an ingenious and quick-witted fellow. The youth paid careful attention to the customs of his trade, and soon he was as adroit and knew as much as anyone.

When they came into Warsaw, he inquired among the people of the city what reputation his merchant enjoyed among them. He learned that the merchant was a respected and honest man, but also that his business was held to be difficult because he undertook many trade journeys to remote lands. As the clever man went about the city thus, he saw the servants in the storehouse, and their smart dress and dignified appearance struck his eyes. Then he decided to give up his service and hire himself out to a trader who owned an important load in the storehouse. As is the custom, he first had to perform tiresome labor for paltry wages. But that did not annoy him; soon he won the confidence of his master and had a part in the conduct of the business until he was fully acquainted with it. When he noted one day, however, that there was nothing more for him to learn here, he took his leave and attached himself to a train of merchants that was going to London. He kept his eyes wide open and let none of the clever and ingenious customs that he saw everywhere escape him, and in whatever one country excelled the others, he had that shown to him and took it in.

Thus he traveled to many kingdoms—England, Germany, France, Spain—and finally came to Italy. There he saw remarkably fine and artistic products of the guild of goldsmiths, the like of which he had not perceived in any other country, and since the opportunity was favorable to him, he set his dexterity and enthusiasm to acquiring this craft. It did not take long before his hands brought to the light of day work so elegant that the oldest masters of the city had to confess that their lives had not succeeded in producing such.

When he had gone so far that there was no longer anyone in the land who surpassed him, he decided to give up this craft and acquire a new one that was held to be uncommonly difficult and at the same time was well esteemed. He went to a master who had as yet been unexcelled in the art of carving human heads, animal shapes, and all kinds of beautiful and delightful things in precious stones. Soon his will had conquered this art too, and there was none among his comrades who could compare with him. Still this new accomplishment did not continue to hold its own in his eyes, and since he had now applied his hand to every artistic achievement, he determined to exercise his mind and to fathom the nature of men and of things. He entered a very advanced school where a famous master of the art of healing instructed youths who streamed to him from all countries. There he grasped the wisdom of his teacher with such acuteness that he penetrated the heart of everything in nature and in the soul of man so that nothing withstood him. Finally, a violent disgust at the imperfection of life drove him from place to place, and he nowhere found rest. Then he recalled his old home and decided to turn his steps there again.

Meanwhile the simple youth had entered into apprenticeship with the shoemaker and had toiled for years just to acquire the craft simply and correctly, but he had not succeeded so well even in this. When he had halfway completed a pair of crude boots, he opened his own shop, took a wife and cobbled from then on. But since he understood his craft only poorly, only the poorest people came to him, people who pay but little. Since, in addition, he needed a long time to complete a piece of work, he had to drudge very hard before he had earned that little. Still this laborious and scanty existence did not damage his good disposition, and although he often found no free moment to eat during the whole day, he was nonetheless joyous and in good spirits from morning till evening.

Thus it happened at times that while he drew the thread through the cobbler's wax, he called to his wife, "Woman, put out for me at once the barley-broth!" Then she handed him a piece of dry bread. And while he vigorously consumed it, he said, "Wife, your barley-broth has never been so good as it is today! So, now give me a fine piece of roast!" Then she handed him once more a good slice of bread. When the shoemaker had eaten this too, he cried out, altogether delighted, "Wife, this is the tenderest roast that I have eaten in all my days. Now give me the dessert." And again he received a piece of bread and praised it as the costliest cake. Thus each day he seasoned the scanty bites with gay fancies, and while he ate, he really tasted all the choice dainties of which he spoke. If he was thirsty, he called, "Woman, bring me a glass of wine, but of our best." She placed before him a glass of water; he held it against the light and said, highly pleased, "I wager even the king does not drink clearer wine!" And it seemed to him as if he tasted on his tongue the very finest of beverages.

It was also this way with his clothing. The cobbler and his wife had between them a shabby sheepskin. If it was cold and he wanted to travel across the land, then he said to his wife, "My love, put the pelt on me!" Then he stroked it and said, "Is it not a fine little pelt? And how nicely it keeps me warm!" But if he had to look in somewhere in the city, then he called, "Wife, bring here the cloth mantle!" Then she again put the pelt on him, and he said smiling, "Does not the cloth shine like satin? There is nothing finer than my little mantle!" Thus he also wore the old pelt as a caftan and as a jacket and was altogether of the opinion that in the whole world there was no nobler garment.

But if with great pains he had finished a shoe—and it always turned out quite clumsy and crude—then he called his wife over, "See now, my heart, what a sweet and elegant little shoe that is! Have you ever seen a prettier?"

"Well," said his wife, "if your shoes turn out so splendidly, why do you take only a taler for a pair while every other shoemaker in the place demands double that?"

"Wife," he then laughed, "why do you want to spoil our mood with what others do? Think rather of what I earn from one hand to the other with a single pair of boots." He reckoned what leather and wax and thread cost him, found that barely five groschen remained as pure earnings, and was of the opinion that no other lot was preferable to his own.

The people of the city knew well the cobbler and his foolish ways and made fun of him. It quite often happened that one of them came in only to tease him, but he soon noticed it and gave them no answer save what he constantly replied, "Just don't jest!" If an honest and guileless person asked him a question, he gave him the simple and straightforward information that he wanted. If, however, someone with apparent seriousness wanted to dupe him in order to bring him to foolish talk and to make merry over him, then he said quite gaily, "Ay, friend, just see how foolish I am! You can be a good deal cleverer than I and still be a proper fool."

One day there spread in the city the report that the clever man, who meanwhile had become abroad an enormously rich and wise lord, was going to retire to his native town. When the simple man heard this, he cried hastily, "Wife, bring me at once the best holiday garment in which I may go to meet the friend of my youth and welcome him." His wife put on him the matted pelt, and he ran thus in front of the city gate on the highway just as there drew up a splendid carriage in which sat the clever man, glorious and dignified. The simple man held onto the vehicle and crief joyfully, "Blessed be God who has brought you hither, my brother!" He said many more loving and joyous words and deported himself naïvely and unconcernedly. To the highly educated man this conduct seemed quite foolish; still he remembered the one friendship of his youth, greeted the shoemaker in a friendly way, took him into his carriage and rode with him into the city. But during the long time that had passed while the clever man was far from home, his father had died and the house that he had left behind had, untended, fallen entirely into ruins so that the clever man found no place there where he could live. He had to seek an inn, yet there was none in the whole city that suited his consequence and his habits. But the simple man, after the death of his father, had moved into his father's house, and when he now perceived the distress of his distinguished friend, he sought him out and said to him, "My brother, do me the honor of staying with me. You will find room enough in my house, for my wife and I need only a single room." The clever man consented, and the simple man hurried home, snatched together the best furniture into the room that the friend of his youth would occupy, and bid his wife scour everything bright and make the best possible preparations. Thus the clever man entered the house of the simple one.

The great fame of his wisdom and his untold accomplishments soon spread throughout the whole country. The great and distinguished of the realm hurried thither in order to take delight in the test of his knowledge and his art. A mighty prince gave him the task of making a ring so ingenious that only he could devise it. The clever man made a ring and scratched on it the image of a tree with thousandfold intertwined boughs and branches. The undertaking succeeded both so boldly and so finely that he was sure that even in Italy, where this art was understood as nowhere else, nothing could be set by the side of his work. But the prince was a crude and ignorant man who only knew how to value coarse splendor, and the glorious object found no favor in his eyes. This lack of understanding in the man who had set him this task filled the wise man with fierce chagrin. Another time an eminent man of the kingdom came to him, brought him a jewel in which a picture was carved, and requested of him that he transfer the design to another jewel, entirely like it in form and color. He tackled the work, and it turned out so well that after its completion none could distinguish the original image from the imitation. All were full of the highest praise; only his own heart was reluctant, for he knew of a tiny, almost invisible defect in one place which had not turned out fully in agreement with the model. Although no one was in a position to point out to him this deficiency, the lonely knowledge gnawed at his soul.

No less unhappy experiences were brought to him by his art of healing. Sick people streamed to him in bands. Then it happened once that a very sick man was brought to him whose suffering no doctor in the land had been able to relieve. Now the wise man possessed a wonderfully effective medicine which he was certain would work the cure. But the relatives of the sick man employed the remedy in an entirely perverted manner so that he died of it. Thereupon they raised a great outcry and a great hatred against the doctor and reproached him with having killed the sick man. In another case the same remedy had produced the desired effect for the same illness, and behold, the convalescent had then boasted that it was not the strange wise man and his potion, but his own strong constitution that had saved him. Thus the art of healing only brought sheer vexation to the clever man.

But even his daily life was in no better plight. Thus it happened one day that he needed a garment, and he sent for the best tailor in the town to whom he gave exact instructions as to the nature of the costume. The master took many pains so that it would turn out well, and in general the result was excellent. Only the cuff of the sleeve had not been made entirely as the wise man had deemed proper and had desired, and this circumstance enraged the learned man, for he was anxious lest in Spain he would perhaps be derided on account of this improperly sewn sleeve cuff, even though here in this country the people understood little enough about suitable clothing.

But the simple man was all the time in good spirits and ran in and out of the room of the clever man with jokes and laughter, which at times furiously annoyed the latter. It did not long remain concealed from the shoemaker, however, how dejectedly his rich friend lived, and so he said to him one day, "How then is it possible that you with your wisdom and your riches continually are at loggerheads with trouble and distress while I, a poor, simple man, live my days peaceful and joyous? Perhaps you would be happier if, like me, you had been placed in the world innocent and with little understanding."

"Good friend," laughed the clever man, "it might after all fall to my portion that sickness should overtake me and destroy my understanding so that I should become like you. But you need have no fear that my wisdom might ever befall you so that you would have to live like me, for such a thing cannot happen now or ever."

It was customary in the city to call the poor cobbler nothing other than "The Simple One" and his rich comrade nothing other than "The Clever One," and by these nicknames they were also registered in the book in which all the inhabitants of the place were described by name and position. Now it happened once that the king of the country turned over the leaves of this book and thus learned that in one city of his country there were two men of whom one was simply called "The Clever One" and the other simply

82

"The Simple One." Then there awoke in him the desire to make the acquaintance of the two, and he communicated to his attendants the wish that these two men be invited to visit him. But he soon asked himself, "Will not both of them be afraid when they suddenly receive a message from their king? The wise man, out of respect, will not know what he ought to answer, and the simpleton in the end will merely play the fool. It would, therefore, be well if I chose two of my courtiers, a clever one for the message to the clever man and a simple one that he might know how to deal with the simple man, and sent them to the governor of that province of my kingdom. I shall have my intention made known to him so that he may show the messengers the proper way to approach these two. Then the messengers would not even tell them that the king commands them to come, but that they would please him if they did so."

A clever man was easily found at this court, but it was difficult to procure a simple one, for where in all the world would such a man be tolerated in the vicinity of a king? Indeed, in the whole of the king's city there was hardly one to be found. The search had already grown troublesome to the ruler and his counselors when it struck them that one simple man actually lived among them, namely, the king's treasurer;

for of all the offices of the court his was the only one
that could certainly not be entrusted to a clever man
since he could easily have administered it more to his
own use and profit than to that of the kingdom. So
the king's treasurer and one of his wise counselors
were dispatched as messengers.

They came to the governor, informed him of the
king's will and inquired concerning the two people.
The governor marveled and said to them, "He whom
you call 'The Clever One' is, in truth, a most remarkably wise and experienced man, and he who is called
by the name of 'The Simple One' is the most miserable
fool that ever existed." At this moment the story of
the pelt, which everyone knew, came into his head;
he told it to the messengers so that they might get a
picture of the limited understanding of the shoemaker.
Then he had someone fetch a splendid garment to
send to the simple man so that his coarse clothes might
not injure the eye of the king.

The treasurer drove to the neighborhood of the
shoemaker, sought his house, entered it and handed
him the royal epistle. But the simple man returned
the letter to him and said, "Know, then, that I am not
versed in reading. You must report to me what is
written here, if you will, so that I may learn it."

"The sense of the writing," the treasurer answered

him, "is that the king invites you to come to him, for he has heard of you and desires to make your acquaintance."

That seemed most remarkable to the shoemaker and he was afraid that someone might be pulling his leg. Therefore he said naïvely, "Just don't jest!"

"Really, no jest!" the messenger assured him.

Then the joy of the simple man was overpowering. He danced around the room and cried out, "Wife, think, what good fortune, the king calls me to him!" He climbed into the carriage quite joyously. When the costly clothes were handed to him, however, he resisted them and would not allow them to be put on him, for he wanted to appear before the king in his beloved, wondrously beautiful pelt.

But while the two were on the trip to the court, the king was besieged by all kinds of complaints about the personality and activities of the governor who had misused his office and had seriously harmed the country through all kinds of intrigues and artifices. The prince was furious at the evildoer and still more at his own counselors who had praised this man as a model of wisdom and prudent conduct, and he called out, "You are all too clever for me, and you have injured me beyond limits with your cleverness!" When the advisers murmured, the king grew still more irritated and shouted, "I shall make the simplest man the governor, for his foolishness cannot do harm if he is only honest and has a straightforward spirit." As he spoke thus, he recalled that the simple man whom he had sent for must already be on the way to where the governor lived, and he decided to confer this honor on precisely this man. He sent thither and commanded that the simple man be received with great honor, and that the wisest and most respected citizens welcome him as their superior.

When the shoemaker had ridden there with his companion of the road, all took place as the king had commanded. The simple man, however, received with great astonishment all the pomp and festivity with which he was met and called out, as usual, "Just don't jest!" But soon he was convinced that the honor really was intended for him. As governor, he now conducted himself simply and honestly, as he had at the time when he had been a poor shoemaker, and since he himself had passed his life without intrigues, he knew how to see into the heart of right and wrong, and his judgments became respected everywhere. His people and his advisers came to love him, and his fame soon penetrated to the king who wished for nothing so fervently as to have at his side a man of such strict virtue and simple understanding. Thus it came about that he appointed the simple man as his prime minister and had a palace built for him not far from his court.

When the king's other messenger came to the clever man and delivered his information, the latter said to him, "Let us, like reasonable men, not hasten unduly. Stay this night with me so that we may consider everything well and deliberate together." At mealtime, after the clever man had discoursed penetratingly on many subjects, he came to the message of the king and spoke as follows, "Who am I that a mighty king desires to see me? Does he not have enough noble vassals and profound counselors at his court that he should send for me?" Now he reflected long within himself over his own words and finally cried out, "It is impossible, you must recognize, that a king could do the like. Evil-minded men have deluded you when they bid you come to me with this message. The truth is that the king does not exist at all. Or have you perhaps received the letter that you brought me from his hand?"

"No," replied the messenger, "I must confess to you that I received it not from the king himself but from one of his officers."

"Have you ever caught sight of his face, then?" the clever man pursued.

"You seem to be little acquainted with the customs

of kings," answered the ambassador. "Otherwise you would know well that they rarely show themselves to the people, and when they do, they are so surrounded by their attendants that it is difficult to catch sight of the king."

"If you consider the matter rightly," the clever man then said, "you will perceive how your own words prove that I am right. For if you, who administer an important office at court, have not seen the king, then who should have, indeed?"

"But who then leads the country?" asked the latter.

To this the clever man replied, "Mark what I say to you, for I am widely traveled and highly experienced. Look, in the country of Italy, sixty noble men rule the kingdom; they are selected by the people, and they share in the conduct of state affairs. There every worthy and meritorious citizen can attain to authority. But here the high officers and courtiers undoubtedly govern; they make the law and do what pleases them. But if the people ask, 'Who demands this of us?' then they answer, 'Why, your king, and it is up to you to obey him.' Thus they command according to their wills, and the king is nothing but an empty name that they have invented in order to frighten and subdue the people." The speech began to impress the messenger, and doubt grew strong within him. But his learned host talked on, "I could bring forward much of that nature, but wait until tomorrow; then I hope to convince you."

The next morning they arose early and the two of them went to the market place. There they met a soldier, and the clever man addressed him thus, "My dear friend, tell me, whom do you serve?"

"Now," he answered, "whom indeed does a soldier serve? The king, I should think!"

"Have you served long?" asked the wise man.

"Indeed," he said, "I have fought faithfully for my lord in many battles, and I regard no calling as higher than mine, to hold high the banner of the king."

"No doubt you know your king well," said the clever man, "since you love him so?"

"I have never seen him," replied the latter sorrowfully, "although it has been my life's dearest wish."

The clever man said to his companion, "Is there a greater foolishness than to shed one's blood for someone who does not exist? And believe me, the whole people is laboring under such a delusion."

The messenger let himself be convinced by his comrade, and when the former said to him, "If you are willing to go with me into the world, then I shall reveal to you the petty minds and perverted opinions of men everywhere," he was ready at once, and the two men departed from there.

Wherever they came, they were not able to see anything other than madness and delusion. The discovery that no king could exist had become for them the maxim and measure for everything, and they would say, "This is just as true as that there is a king." While they wandered thus through the lands of all rulers and took no interest in anything save in blemishes of the human spirit, they left their external circumstances of fortune so wholly unattended, that soon they had bitter experience of life's need and were forced to give up their horses and all else that they had brought with them just in order to obtain a meager subsistence. Thus exposed to every misfortune of poor wanderers, they nonetheless marched indefatigably onward and gathered an ever greater store of melancholy experiences. But finally they decided to return home in order to turn their treasure of knowledge to good account and to bring it to the people.

Thus they came into the city where the poor shoemaker now resided as prime minister. As they were marching through the streets of the city, they observed before an unpretentious little house a huge throng of people who had gathered about a row of carriages, princely coaches and wretched village carts mixed together. As they drew nearer, they glimpsed in each vehicle an infirm or sick person who waited eagerly to gain entrance through the low door of the little house. Other men came out with shining countenances and joyous praises for the helpful man who, through his sincere encouragement and the kind strength of his blessed nature, brought the sick great relief in their suffering and to many complete recovery. The clever man thought at first that a famous doctor dwelt here, but he learned to his amazement that this healer was not learned, but instead enjoyed in the mouth of the people the reputation of a wonder-worker. He broke out into angry laughter and said to his companion, "Have we, therefore, traveled through the whole world only to find the greatest of all follies at the threshold of our home? Brother, you must recognize that this is a gross impostor who draws the money out of the pockets of the ignorant people."

They turned away and went further, and since they had not eaten for a long time and were hungry, they gathered together the last groschen in their pockets and entered the next eating-house in order to have a meal there. While they ate, they ridiculed in a loud and unseemly manner the undertakings of the wonder-worker so that the innkeeper behind the bar noticed them and listened with annoyance to their talk. Since it was about noon, the dining room soon filled with guests who heard with indignation the words of the two men, and when the son of the wonder-worker then entered and had to be a witness to their banter, the innkeeper became angry and threw them both out, and the people fell on them and thrashed them soundly. The two clever men fled from there and hastened to the municipal guard to seek protection and justice. When the captain of the municipal guard had learned for what reason the two had been mistreated, he flew at them, loaded them with insults, and finally shoved them out. For he too believed in the wonder-worker, who had saved his very sick child for him.

The two now went from court to court and everywhere raised their complaints, but the wonder-worker was honored in all places. They were repulsed one time after another and received only bitter words and cudgelings on the way. Finally they came before the palace of the minister and asked the guard to admit them, for a great wrong had been done to them. They were brought before the minister, and this man, who had once been called "The Simple One," recognized immediately in the wretched and exasperated wanderer the comrade of his youth. But the latter did not recognize in the minister the needy cobbler, for he bore his post with great dignity. The minister made himself known, greeted his former friend with cordial mien, and asked him what he desired. The clever man related that he had been cruelly beaten for the sake of an impostor, which is what this wonder-worker was who led the whole city by the nose. The minister smiled, comforted him, and requested him first to go with his companion into the bath where servants awaited them and would give them decent clothes. After that he invited them to eat with him.

At the table the clever man, who was greatly astonished by the altered character and circumstances of his friend, asked him, "My dear friend, how did you come then to this position of dignity?"

"My lord, the king, conferred it on me," replied the minister.

"What," said the clever man, "you too are gripped by this madness and believe in a king! I tell you there is no king."

"How can you suggest so monstrous a thing?" cried the minister. "I see the king's face daily."

"What makes you think," jeered the clever man, "that he with whom you speak is actually the king? Were you intimate with him from childhood on? Did you know his father and grandfather and can say that they were kings? Men have told you that this is the king. They have fooled you."

Then the minister said to him, "So, do you still continue, then, to live in your subtleties and not see life? You asserted once that it would be easier for you to decline into my simplicity than for me to rise to your cleverness. No, you will never receive the grace of simplicity!"

# THE KING'S SON
# AND THE
# SON OF THE MAID

Many hundreds of years ago there ruled far from here a great king who governed benevolently a broad and fruitful land. In his palace was a maidservant who performed faithful service for the queen, and the queen's heart was well disposed toward her. She was girdle maid to the queen and had only easy duties.

The day came when the queen was to bear a child, and at the same hour this was also going to happen to the maid. The servant fetched a wise woman who, because of her sagacity and her secret arts, enjoyed a great reputation in the land. She lifted the son of the king to the light and also delivered the son of the maid. Then she wrapped the king's child in coarse linen and laid it next to the sleeping maid, but the child that the maid had borne as the son of a servant she swaddled in soft silk and made up a bed for it on the couch of the queen. When the mothers woke up, each fondled the child in her arm.

The boys grew up handsome and strong. The son of the servant was honored in the palace and elevated above all the sons of the land. He was the first after the king and sat on a silver seat beside the throne. He was instructed in all that in which the wise men of the land and the counselors were versed. But the son of the king blossomed under the roof of a servant, and the bottom of his heart and his bright eyes were the sole sources of his wisdom. Although he called a lowly man father, one discovered in him a proud manner and a free nature. Above all he loved the lonely paths of the mountains and shunned the companionship of the noisy. But to the boy who stayed in the palace, the splendor of the king's hall seemed cold; he often looked out at the countryside into which two columns opened, and his heart drew him to the farmer who cut through the black earth with his plow.

The wise woman lived in a hut outside the city, where the forest began. She bore the burden of many decades and knew that her death drew near. Her breathing was oppressed by the secret that she had exchanged the king's son with the son of the maid, and it pained her to conceal it forever. She went to the window of her hut and whispered it cautiously so that no one heard it except the wind which moved the leaves of the birches. The wind, however, bore it hurriedly to the women and children who sought shade and sweet berries in the forest. The women told it at home to their husbands, and each husband confided it at evening drink to his dearest friend. But the men of the city spoke thus with one another: "Let us guard this secret carefully from the king so that misfortune and doubt may not visit his old age! For what has taken place cannot be corrected. Shall we one day set over us as king the youth who grew up in a lowly house? And may not the whole thing be a lie and an idle tale?"

There was one in their midst, nonetheless, who went and betrayed the secret to the king's false son. "Know that many among the people regard you as the son of the maid," he said, "and the time might easily come, I think, when the country will rebel against you and raise that one to your place if you do not take care in good time that he be destroyed." When the king's false son heard this, he went into the darkest chamber of his castle and pondered evil thoughts. From that hour on his ill humor never left him. He rode out in the gray of the morning with his suite and trampled underfoot the seed on the fields of the man who was in reality his father. Henceforth, he did him whatever injury he could.

The time came when the king died, and the king's false son ascended the throne and governed the land. The servant he oppressed ever more cruelly. But the latter understood well why this happened to him. He spoke now to his foster child, who was, in reality, the king's son, and told him what the people said of him, and how the king had come to hate him. "See, I have great pity for you," he continued. "If you are my son, how should I not be sad since that one will destroy you? But if you are the king's son, as they say, then such a fate, indeed, is not due you. Therefore, flee out of the country." The youth sank into melancholy and knew not what to do. But the king did not desist from persecuting him with wrongs of all kinds so that he was at last willing to flee. His foster father gave him what gold he possessed and had good clothes made for him. Sadly the youth went out of the land.

Abroad he spent his days in idleness, drank away his money in the evenings with the young people in the taverns, and threw it to the dancers. But his heart remained heavy.

Meanwhile the false king governed his land harshly and mercilessly. When he went with gloomy countenance through the streets of his city and all bowed before him, he always imagined that he heard a whisper from the crowd calling him the son of the servant. He turned away darkly and inflicted new hardships on his people.

One day he went hunting with his suite. They came to a place so delightful that the king wished to pause there. He laid himself to rest under a tree. The tree stood in blossom and bent its branches above clear water. There the king was overcome by pangs of conscience that he had committed an injustice and driven away an innocent man. It disturbed him and destroyed all his pleasure. He bid his people return. But when he was again lodged in the palace, he thrust this anxiety from him and acted as before.

In the same period of time, the king's true son one night had a wonderful dream. He saw a market before him, and he was commanded in sleep to go to this market; there someone would approach him and offer him work which he should accept even if it seemed to him difficult and menial. He awoke, and the dream had penetrated deep into his soul. He drove it out of his thoughts, nonetheless, and lived in sport and revel, as before. But the dream befell him another time and ever again and at last weighed heavily on his spirits. One night in the dream he heard a voice say, "Have pity on yourself and do as is commanded you." In the gray of the day he raised himself from his bed, wrapped himself in the simple garment of a servant, gave away to the people in the inn what remained of his possessions, and walked out of the city the way the voice had indicated to him. After he had been under way a good while, he saw in the distance a market and recognized again the place of the dream. As he set foot in the market place, a merchant came toward him and addressed him thus, "If you desire work, then hire yourself out to me as cattle drover. I still have need of one." It seemed hard to the youth, but the dream ruled him, and he agreed. The merchant bid him go now here and now there and gave him orders in the manner of a rough master. He rode near the herd and punished the inattentive drover with cruel blows of his stick.

Once they marched through a thick, dark forest. There two beasts detached themselves from the herd of the youth and disappeared between the trees which stood so thick that it seemed as if they had intertwined their branches into a single great crown. The merchant let fly at him as if he wanted to kill him. The youth hurried after the animals, and since in the thicket they again and again showed themselves and then escaped his gaze, he penetrated ever deeper into the forest. When he halted at last exhausted, he saw

100

that night had settled in the forest. The horror of the wilderness descended on him; the dreadful roaring of the beasts of prey pressed in upon him. He spent the night in the strong boughs of a tree.

When he looked about him in the morning, his two animals stood peacefully under the tree. He climbed down in order to seize them, but when he wanted to lay his hand on them, they again fled and again he pursued them. At times they tarried in a clearing to eat some grass; but when he came there, they fled and drew him deeper into the wood. He followed them into the thickest center of the forest where live the wild animals who know no fear since they are far from the dwelling places of men. Night again came on, and the cries of the wilderness clamored horribly about his ears. He climbed a very high tree and, behold, there lay a man. He was frightened; but since he perceived that it was a being like himself, he was glad no longer to be alone, and he asked the other, "Who are you, man?"

"Who are *you*, man?" responded the other, "And where have you come from?"

The youth informed him, "Two animals that strayed from the herd have drawn me here, but tell me, how have *you* come here?"

"My horse brought me to this place," the other answered. "I descended in order to rest; then the animal ran away. I chased after him, was not able to catch him and finally came here." Now they talked the matter over and agreed that they would keep together.

But when the night began to yield to the dawn, the voice of a powerful laugh resounded threateningly over the forest and made them tremble. Like a storm wind, it gripped the tree on which the two lay, bowed it to the ground and snapped it again into the air.

Then the comrade of the youth said, "I have been many days and nights at this place, and each time darkness begins to disappear, this laugh roars over the wood."

"This is evidently a place of spirits," answered the youth, "for never in the kingdom of men is a voice like this heard."

Soon after it became daylight, and behold, there stood the animals of the youth under the tree, and the horse of his companion had also made his appearance. They descended to the ground, the animals again escaped, each man followed his own into the forest, and so they wandered apart from each other. As the youth ran, he suddenly saw something lying at his feet, and when he bent down he saw it was a sack filled with fine fresh bread. He appeased his hunger and was joyful, for what better could he find in the wilderness? When he had satisfied himself, he took the sack on his shoulders and followed the animals further.

Where the forest issued into the deepest darkness and became so thick that one could not extricate oneself, he met on his way a man of a stranger appearance than any other being he had ever seen. Tangled, red-brown hair fluttered like flames around his earth-gray face in which lay deeply embedded two green eyes like two balls of malachite. His clothes appeared to have been made out of the skins of a thousand lizards. He cast his gaze on the youth with such penetrating eyes that the latter, transfixed, could not move from the spot.

The wood creature addressed him, "How have you come hither? Never yet has one from the kingdom of men reached this place."

Then the youth noticed that his companion was no man. But the wood spirit asked once again, "What do you seek here?"

"I am chasing two animals that have strayed from my herd," he replied.

"Enough," said the wood spirit, "now come with me."

The youth went behind him and dared not address

him. On the way he met his comrade of the night and made a sign to him to come with them.

Then the latter noticed the sack with bread on his shoulders and entreated, "My brother, I have not eaten for so many days, give me bread."

"How can I give you my bread?" the youth replied. "Consider, how will I save my own life in this wilderness?"

But the other pressed him hard and said, "I shall give myself to you completely as your servant if you will give me bread."

Then the youth took him as his servant, the latter swore with an oath that he would never leave him, and the youth shared with him as much of the bread as he could eat.

They now followed the wood spirit together. Finally they came out of the forest into a dismal valley. The ground was covered with snakes and salamanders which rolled their slimy, slippery bodies over one another.

The youth asked the wood spirit, "How shall we get through here?"

The latter pointed silently to a house that stood high over their heads in the air. Then he seized them in his hands, rose with them into the air and brought them unmolested into his house. This was crammed with bizarre furnishings whose significance the youth did not know, but he discovered all therein that a human being needed. The wood spirit set on the table good things aplenty for them to eat and drink and left the house as he had come. The two remained and satiated themselves.

Then the servant was very vexed that he had sold himself for the sake of a single hour, for now he had food in abundance. He sighed and groaned aloud, "How do I come to such a life? How do I come to be a servant?"

"From what position then do you come here," the youth asked him, "that it vexes you so to serve?"

To this the latter replied and told him how he had been a king in the realm of men, and how it had been rumored among the people that the true king had been exchanged after birth and lived in the house of a servant while he, the servant's son, sat on the throne; and how, since then, he had done much evil to that person until he fled the country. And he told further that one night a dream had befallen him and the voice of the dream had commanded him, "Cast your kingship from you and go hence where your eyes lead you, for you must atone for your guilt." He had not heeded the dream, but it always came again; he had not found rest on any night until at last he did as he was bid,

forsook the kingship and went hence; and now he
had become a servant.

The youth took in all this and said nothing. At twilight the wood spirit came, handed them food and
drink and prepared a couch for them. Toward morning the voice of the powerful laugh again resounded
over the forest. The servant urged the youth to ask
the wood spirit what that was. So he asked him,
"What is this voice that roars over the forest in the
early morning?"

"That," said the spirit, "is the laughter with which
the day derides the night when at the approach of
dawn she asks him, 'Why do I no longer have a name
when you come?' Then day breaks out in laughter
and takes possession of the earth."

After he had said this, he left them as before. Only
at evening did he return. In the night they heard, in
a mighty swelling, the voices of all the forest animals;
they recognized the roar of the lion, the horrible howl
of the roaming leopard, the sweet cooing of the wood
doves and the cry of the stag, and ever new voices
mingled in. At first, it all sounded to them like a great
confusion; but as they inclined their ear to it more,
they perceived that it was the tune of a song. All the
happiness of the earth seemed to them vain compared
with the blessing of this melody. The servant per-

suaded his master to ask the wood spirit what this was, and he did so.

"The animals of the wood," answered the wood spirit, "have learned that the sun has made a present to the moon of a new silver garment. And since the moon is their great benefactor and its light is strewn over their nocturnal paths (for the animals of the forest hide themselves by day and are awake at night), they have decided to honor it with a new song, and they have devised the melody that you have heard." Since they marveled at this, he continued, "If this already appears incomprehensible to you, how much more will you be astonished when you see my wonderful staff in which resides the power that causes each animal that one touches with it to sing this melody!"

On the third morning the wood spirit led them out of his house through the air to the forest path where he had found them, and said to them, "Return now into the realm of men!"

"Which way shall we turn?" asked the youth.

"Seek the country," replied the wood spirit, "that is called the foolish country with the wise king!" And he showed them the direction. But in departing he handed the youth as a gift the wonderful staff of which he had spoken, bid him be of good spirit, and vanished.

So they set out then on the way. They entered the province of men and went onward until they reached the country that was called the foolish country with the wise king. The country was surrounded by a wall, and they had to go around many miles before they came to the gate. When they wanted to enter, the gatekeeper refused to admit them.

Then the youth cried out, "That is, in truth, a foolish land that admits no travelers!"

The man at the gate replied to him, "Up till now our land was called the foolish country with the wise king. But now our king has died, and at his death he commanded that after him the land should be called the wise country with the foolish king until one should come who might undertake through his wisdom to restore the earlier name, and he should become king in his stead. Therefore, we admit no one unless he will venture on such an undertaking. If you are ready to do this, then enter."

This the youth did not dare and withdrew with sunken head. The servant advised that they should travel to another country, for here they could not remain. But the youth would not do so, for he recalled the words of the wood spirit. Meanwhile, they were joined by a man in black clothes who sat on a black horse. He rode up to them and gazed at the youth, who under this gaze felt remarkably as though he were compelled to touch the horse with his staff. He did so, and the horse began to sing the moon melody in an exquisite voice.

Then the man in black laughed and said, "Will you forever merely play games with your staff? And has it not struck you that it was bestowed on you for something better? Has it not become clear to you that this instrument entices out of each being the very voice of his heart and that, as long as you possess it, you can understand each thing from its heart?" After these words the stranger turned his horse and rode away.

Then the youth understood why the wood spirit had directed him here. He turned back to the gate, demanded admission and agreed to undertake the task. The watchman led him to the assembly of princes. They sat about in a circle in the hall of the king and did not know what to do.

The princes spoke to him, "Know that we too are no fools, but the dead king was a man of such great wisdom that we all are regarded merely as fools compared to him; therefore, they named the land the foolish country with the wise king. The king left behind him a son; he too is wise, but only so little that compared to us he is a fool; and for this reason the old king in dying commanded that the name of the land should be turned around until one came who should resemble him in wisdom and would restore the first name. To him who can do this, his son will yield the dominion. Know therefore, youth, what you are venturing and that the test is difficult. In our city is a garden which was founded in ancient times by a family of giants. Out of its black earth on a broad field there grow, like trees, powerful weapons of steel and martial implements of gold and silver. But if a man sets foot in the garden, then the spirits of the departed family of giants arise and pursue him and he is put to flight. Now let us see whether you, by chance, are so wise that you can master the spirits."

The youth had the way to the garden shown him. About it was built a wall; a rusty gate hung open at the hinges; no watchman was to be seen. In a niche in the wall next to the gate there stood behind a silver grating the statue of a man with a golden crown and golden mantle of a king but with face and hands of ivory. Above the statue had been set in the wall an alabaster tablet upon which, in shining letters, these words were to be read: "He who stands here was a king of this country in days of yore, and before him and after him there was incessant war, but in his days was peace." The youth touched the grating, and it immediately sprang open. Then he understood that he was bidden to expel the spirits and redeem the garden by means of this king. He seized the statue, strode with it into the garden, and placed it in the center. Nothing stirred and he came out of the garden in peace. Then he went and told this to the princes. They came there, and he led them into the pacified garden.

"Although we have seen this," the princes said to him, "we cannot yet give the kingdom to you for the sake of this one deed. You must pass a second test. Since olden times there has been in our country a finely carved throne, in a marble colonnade, erected on a hill in the center of the kingdom. The seat is carved out of the wood of a holy tree and adorned with the shapes of all the animals and plants that are in the country. Before it stands a table and on it a candelabrum with seven arms. Formerly it used to be that everyone who sat on the throne surveyed the whole land, and no act that took place in it remained hidden from him. And he who kindled the seven arms of the candelabrum knew all the thoughts that were thought anywhere in the country. But since the death of the old king, the eyes of him who sits on the throne have become clouded, and he no longer sees what surrounds him, and the candelabrum no

111

longer burns when one wants to kindle it. But from
the throne there proceed many roads, like the rays
of a star, in all directions throughout the whole land.
In the midst of each road there stands a winged,
golden animal. Formerly all these animals sang at midnight a wonderful melody. But since the death of the
old king they remain silent. If a man approaches them,
they fling open their jaws and devour him. The people
live in anxiety and dismay, and no one up till now
has fathomed the origin of this thing. Now we shall
see whether you are so wise that you can restore the
old order."

They led him into the hall to the throne. When he
looked at it, he recognized that it was carved out of
the same wood as the staff that the wood spirit had
given him. He observed the throne in order to discover through what means it had lost its power. Then
he noticed that on the corner of the throne a carved
rose was missing; he sought and found it hidden under
a stone of the hall. He inserted it again into the throne.
Then he observed the candelabrum and found that
it had been displaced a little from the center of the
table, and he brought it to its proper position. Now
he ascended the throne and kindled the candelabrum.
He surveyed the whole land and all thoughts and
deeds, past and present, and he recognized that before

his death the old king had intentionally disarranged everything so that the man might be found who could restore it and bring each thing to its proper place. He saw the golden animals standing on the roads and noticed that they too had been moved a little from their position. He had each animal moved back to its old place, and the animals let men approach them unharmed. When the last animal came to his place, it was midnight, and all began to sing the great melody.

Then the princes gave the kingship to the youth. But he said to his servant, "Now I understand that I am, in truth, the king's son and you are, in truth, the son of the maid."

# THE
# MASTER OF PRAYER

There once lived a man who was called the master of prayer. He served God all the days of his life with praise and possessed in this deed a strength such as had never yet arisen in the soul of a man. He had chosen his place of habitation far from the dwellings of the earthly on a silent sea, shaded round by trees. At times it happened that he made ready, left the abode of his concentration and visited the world. Then he attached himself to one person or another whom he met by chance, exchanged address and rejoinder with him, and, ascending from conversation about everyday matters with the companion who was beginning to trust him, uplifted his soul and gradually led it to the meaning of all being. And many a time it happened that the ear and heart of the other opened to him and allowed his word to enter, and this man quickly renounced all ties and all lust for life and

**115**

followed him. Thus a settlement grew on the shore of the sea and solidified itself. But the master knew quite well what each one of his followers needed in order to give him the impulse to holy flight, and so he let the rich live meagerly so that the simple spirit might awaken in them, but to him who had been a beggar he granted a plentiful sufficiency.

Meanwhile there arose in the provinces of men a complaint about those who had disappeared, and soon traps were set for the strange man on all the roads. But no one was ever able to catch him. He worked unhindered with his word and led away those who had become his.

At the same time there existed in the sphere of the world a land that was called the country of wealth after the nature of its inhabitants. They saw in money alone the goal of their life and would recognize no other profit and no other perfection than possession. Thus all posts of honor and all ranks among them were regulated by this valuation. It was necessary to own a certain amount in order merely to be a man; he who did not possess this much stood lower and occupied in their esteem the rank of a manlike animal, and was called such. He who owned more than that minimum amount occupied a higher position, and a very rich man stood near the stars; for he had, so they believed, the power of the stars, which cause gold to grow in the bowels of the earth. But the richest of all, who could never grasp all that was theirs or even merely survey it, these they exalted to gods above them and served them in the dust. It was ordered that each show his possessions every year so that he could maintain his station, rise, or fall, and it was then possible at times that from a man, an animal would come into being, and from an animal, a man.

They had determined order, law, and government in such a manner, in accordance with their belief, and had chosen to find in this the only meaning and true essence of existence. Their pride, consequently, grew beyond measure, and finally they discovered that it was not suitable to their nobility to remain among the ordinary living beings, and they moved together into a mountain on the edge of the earth, for they believed that it behooved them to dwell higher than the rest of the peoples of the earth and to look down on them. So in individual groups they peopled the mountain tops, blocked up the roads that led from them into the world, and left to each mountain only *one* secret approach. This hidden path they manned with guards whom they selected from among the poor, for these were not compromising their station too much if they had to stay on the road to the despised sphere of the world.

In this country, however, everything became wilder and more disorderly. Robbery and murder prevailed everywhere as the great means to perfection, but compassion was regarded as shameful madness. One brought human animals for sacrifices to the richest, who were held to be gods, and many a person did not hesitate to sacrifice to them his own life, for through this he hoped in his next reincarnation also to appear as a rich man and a god.

But the master of prayer came to know about this country. A profound sympathy for the poor fools at once overwhelmed him, and he determined to use all his power to set them right. So he betook himself there, sought out the guards and spoke to them of the vanity of money and of the true meaning of the world. But they paid no attention to him; for even though they were poor and worthless, still the doctrine of the divinity of gold had become deeply rooted in their hearts. So the master left them then, altered his appearance, and secretly found his way into the country. There he soon tried again to penetrate into the benumbed souls of the people, but all his inner strength was powerless, and he had to go away without success but with the intention of returning soon for new struggle.

In those days there sojourned on earth a powerful hero whose deed was conquest and who desired to subjugate all countries to himself. Many countries were already subject to him, and their inhabitants lived peacefully under his protecting hand. He who surrendered to him suffered no injury to possession and life, but he who dared to resist him, he destroyed. He would send ahead messengers to every country that he approached on his march to order submission, and only if they had refused to submit did he subdue the people with his armies and make them subject to him.

Now it happened that the people in the country of the rich learned through merchants, who had been sent by them into the despised remainder of the world to collect new treasures for their great, that this conqueror was on the way to their kingdom and proposed to conquer it. A terrible anxiety overwhelmed them. It was not the new government that they feared so much. But they had learned that the hero prized gold little, in fact, despised it and would not tolerate that one honor its possession. Thus it was their belief and their order of life that had to be defended from attack. A great council of the people was convened.

Here the merchants, who had looked around in all the breadth of the earth, gave report of a country whose wealth far surpassed their own, in fact, surpassed any human conception, so that all its inhabitants were gods in might through their possessions. Surely, they now imagined, these people held the means of help in their gold-filled hands.

But while the council met, the master of prayer had again made his way into this strange land. Like the first time, he began to talk with the guards, and they told him how an invincible hero threatened their province and how their great men intended to send to the land of gods for help against the oncoming warrior. Laughing he rebuked them for such folly and spoke to them of God, the source and goal of all inner life. This time the guards followed his speech with half an ear, and at the end one of them said, "And what then can I do who am just an individual and a powerless man!" It seemed to the master then as if, with this answer, a great event had already taken place.

He went further into the city where everywhere he heard talk of the warrior and of the danger that threatened the faith. He mingled among all kinds of people, listened to them, and sought to show them the futility of their way of thinking. While they gave him reports of the hero and his deeds, he said to himself once, "Can it be *he?*"—and it was as if he knew him. This was noticed by some who were already provoked with him because he ridiculed their law; they seized him on the spot and brought him before the rulers that they should judge him as a blasphemer of the faith and as one who was in league with their adversary. The judges interrogated him as to whether he knew that conqueror.

"I once served a king," answered the master. "At his court there lived a hero. If, as I believe, it is this man who threatens your country, then I know him."

"But from where do you know him?" they asked.

Whereupon he commenced and related the following:

"The king of whom I spoke to you possessed a wonderful figure that borrowed its form from a hand with all its folds and furrows. This was a map of all the worlds at all times, and whatever happened stood drawn on it to read, the fate of countries, cities and men and all the pathways to this world and the hidden pathways to distant worlds. There stood each thing as it was at the hour when the world was created, as it has been since then, and as it is today. Thus Sodom is registered in its pride before its destruction, and there is Sodom as it is today, touched by the finger of the Lord. But the king alone could read the hand."

Thus spoke the master, all listened to him, and the ring of truth that sounded in his talk knocked at their hearts.

"Now tell us, where is the king?" they asked further.

But some were seized immediately by their old craving for gold and inquired greedily, "If he is in possession of such wisdom, it may well be that he can show us ways that lead into the bowels of the earth to the place of gold?"

Then the master became angry and cried out, "Do you always think of amassing wealth? Never speak of it to me!"

"Well," they answered, "tell us at any rate where your king resides."

"Today," he said, "even I do not know it. But I shall tell you what took place." And he related this history:

"There were a king and a queen who had an only daughter.

"At the court of the king were masters of many arts and skills. The king, who was lord of the hand, the map of all worlds and times, knew the place where each art and skill had its primal source which flowed out of the depths of eternity; and he knew the ways to these places. If a master came to feel that the grace in him had been exhausted and that things no longer submitted to his command, then the king sent him to his place to renew his might. Thus there was a singer there who had the gift of finding enchanting words and tones and with them moving all hearts. To him the king showed the place of inexhaustible melody that sounds forth from itself back into itself. And there was a wise man whom the king led to the place of light where the last foundations open and no level can withhold itself from the eye. To me he showed the place of the soul where the fountain of fire beat against me, and the power of my prayer was rejuvenated in its stream. And in the same manner that conqueror of whom you are afraid owed to the king the perfection of his invincibility. For he showed him the path to the place where stood in the earth the sword of victory, the sight of which hurls down all living beings that bar its road. And the king gave him the sword. But from time to time he must return to its place and plant the sword in the earth, which nourishes and consecrates it for new wars.

"When now the king's daughter grew up, her father summoned all his followers so that they should advise who should become her husband. My advice was that she should be given to the hero. Thus it happened, and the hero and the princess were married. After a while the king's daughter bore a child that was a sheer miracle of beauty, and a radiance emanated from it. It came into the world with perfected knowledge; only speech was still lacking to it, but from its expression one could read that it understood the inner meaning of every speech. It even looked at the dumb things as if they told it something and laughed at them, not as if succumbing to a whim of the moment but as if out of a great and secret knowledge.

Then it came to pass once that all the king's men were gone at the same time, each to his place to renew his gift. At that time a great storm wind came over the world and in its raging mixed up the elements with one another, made the ocean into mainland and the mainland into ocean and fruitful habitation of men into desert wastes. He also entered the king's palace, roaring, took the marvelously beautiful child of the king's daughter on his wings and bore it away in whirling haste. The king, the queen, and the king's daughter all hurried after him wailing, but in the terrible revolution of the elements none found the road by which the child was taken away, and so they scattered in all directions, straying aimlessly. Meanwhile, one after the other, each of the king's men returned home from his place to the house of the king, and each found it abandoned. And each in his anguish set out to seek the lost ones and did not wait for his comrades. Thus we have all become separated from one another and seek one another in all places."

Thus spoke the master of prayer, and the people heard his words with great astonishment. They deliberated about him and decided not to let him out of the city so that if the hero really proved to be his friend, he could intercede with him for them. For already the hero's messengers had come into the country and demanded submission. Also the great hero himself had marched with his bands nearer and nearer to the country of wealth, and while his messengers still were conferring with the mightiest men of the kingdom, he already lay with his troops before the walls and awaited the decision. When the rich now turned to the master for protection, he said he would go into the camp of the hero to see whether he recognized in him his former friend. He did so, met one of the warriors and began a conversation.

"What are your customs," he asked, "and how did it happen that you made yourselves subject to this man?"

Then the soldier reported how the great event of

that storm wind had befallen the children of the world.

"When the power of the fiend had mitigated itself," he said, "the men stood there helpless and scattered, estranged from their accustomed homesteads. They reflected then that they needed a ruler and pondered on whom they might raise over them as their king. All were agreed that he who stood closest to the meaning of life should be their lord. But about the meaning of life there were many and varied opinions. The men could come to no accord and no conclusion.

"Some thought to find the goal in wisdom; for can one get from all things anything better, they said, than to know them? But others raised the objection that wisdom would be an idle game without the power of words and would waste itself within its own circumference if it were not joined by speech which leads it into the realm of working and happening; the word is the meaning of life. Again there existed a group that declared that all knowing and saying comes from others and goes to others; one thing alone holds sway wholly its own, affected by nothing alien, and that is beauty, which rests eternally in itself. She alone should be sought; she alone should be served. But others among them cried out that beauty would not be at all real without one who rejoices in her; she is nothing other than a thing and image of joy, born mysteriously out of joy, begetting wonderful joy everywhere, embraced by joy; joy is the sun in whose warm light life perfects itself. Still again there were some who listened to this scornfully and with compressed lips, and soon they let it be understood that it was foolish to strive after such fleeting and unstable vanities; the true goal of life is death and to breathe in its atmosphere during all of one's earthly days is the only value of existence. To them, however, some replied that it is only the path of those without deed that is limited by death; but he who creates noble works and wins honor withstands destruction, for he appears as an image to distant generations in the hour of their reflection and makes himself into a never-to-be-extinguished star of future human ages; honor is the meaning of existence for it binds it to eternity.

"In such manner they all disputed about the goal for seven days and seven nights until it became clear to them that there was no bridge from one to the other. Each group set out, one after the other, and each went its way to select a country and a prince in conformity with their view of the meaning of life.

"But I and my comrades," spoke the warrior to the master of prayer, "we were strong men, a great band, but unused to speaking, and we did not take part in the quarrel. Still we could not join any of the peoples, for we felt in our blood and in the beat of our hearts how without force life would lack meaning, and beyond that we could see nothing save to use it and to influence the use of it by others. When the others now departed, we too made ready and marched away, and every creature hid itself when we came. One day a young hero met us and demanded submission. When we refused it, he raised a sword and held it toward us, and the sight of it alone bowed us to the earth. We vowed faithfulness to him, he assumed dominion over us, and since then we march after him, triumphing from country to country. But, strange to say, our lord says that it is not strength and conquest that signifies to him the meaning of life; there is another meaning, and its way leads to another goal. To us, however, his views and his will are dark, although in all this time a love for our lord has touched our hearts and made us see, so that in many things we see what formerly was closed to us, and the world seems to us broader and brighter."

When the master had heard all, he asked to be conducted to the hero. When the two men met, they recognized and embraced each other. But the anguish for the lost ones hovered over them.

"When I returned at that time from my journey

after the storm had laid waste the world," spoke the hero of his fate, "I found my house deserted and all my dear ones vanished from me. Then my steps no longer obeyed the way, but strayed about at random. As I roamed thus, I came to a place where I was certain in my heart that the king must be tarrying, but I could not find him. Then I went further. Another time I sensed the nearness of the queen. And so on my way I have set foot on the abodes of all my dear ones without finding one. But your place I have not seen, and my step has not crossed yours."

"I too," answered the master, "have gone over all the places where those who are dear to us paused to lament, and in each place the lament had lodged in the branches of the trees and in the throats of the birds, and so they rustled and sang it down to me. And over your place too have I been.

"For on a hill there lay spread a golden glaze that did not vanish even in the twilight, and the glaze painted on the stony summit of the hill the shape of a crown. Then I knew that the king had lingered here, and here had lain beside him his crown, which cannot stay at any place without leaving it its image. And from round about there came to me out of the air the mighty and lonesome laments. But I could not find the king's track.

129

"Farther on I went over a sandy country. There I observed on the ground great drops of blood that stayed on the ground, did not trickle away and did not dry, and from them the glance of two eyes seemed to press upward toward me. I knew that these were the tears of the queen which she had wept out of her blood. And through the sand whispered the lament, soft and broken. But the queen was nowhere to be beheld in the wide, open plains.

"I went from there, and one morning I came on a brook over which flowed a thin milky streak that did not mix with the water. And out of the brook there hummed forth, softly and tenderly, a gentle, lamenting cradlesong that never ended, and flowing in even measure seemingly without change, still gave birth to ever new sounds. And I knew that the milk had sprung from the breast of the king's daughter as she stood there and pined for her child. But she herself was not there.

"Later I came upon a gigantic stone in a heath. I sat down next to it and perceived that it was covered with signs. I recognized lines and paths similar to those that were engraved in the mysterious hand that belonged to the king. Here the wise man of the king had been and had sought to imitate some lines from

130

the tablet of the worlds. And also from the dumb stone the lament spoke with soundless voice.

"Another time I walked up a steep grade and reached a place where an abyss opened sightlessly down into the darkness. But the darkness was not empty; rather, a lamenting tone hovered therein, swung back and forth in the space, entangled itself in the limitless and returned. Here the singer of the king had stood, and his song had filled the abyss.

"Then I came to a meadow in which grew a single tree with widespread branches. Underneath it the earth was rooted up, as though from the thrust of an enormous sword. And from the cavity ascended a distant whisper of the lament. Then I recognized your presence.

"But on another day my steps led me into a forest valley. There I saw lying on gray moss a lock of sun-blond hair that shone of its own light. Round about me between the bushes was the gentle tread of the naked feet of a child. But there was no shape amongst them. And in the bushes was a talking, not like a lament, but like the clear and peaceful talking of a child that is certain of all the future. But the talk came from no mouth, rather hung and fluttered over the bushes like gossamer."

"Over all these places I too have gone," replied the

131

hero, "but by the gold hair of my child I have lingered and wept, and seven strands of it I have taken with me. They light up in the seven colors of the rainbow and are my consolation on all my ways.

"When I arose and walked onward, I came on a band of strong people whom I have conquered and at whose head I have set myself in order to conquer the world for my king."

Then the master remembered the people in the country of wealth, and he told the hero of the madness that had befallen them, and how deeply they were possessed by their mania. He confided to the hero that it seemed to him a sheerly impossible undertaking to change their views. "For," he said, "wherever man adheres to being something or doing something, there his roots remain in the human, and out of his roots he can become whole, and in whatever he engages himself, in knowledge or in the word, in beauty or in joy, in death or in eternal honor, he can be saved through himself and can himself establish his life. But where man adheres to the illusion of possessing something, there he tears up his roots out of the human; they no longer draw up healing to him from out of the human earth, and I know no help for him."

"I have heard once from our king," spoke the hero, "that it is possible to liberate men from all errors save from the error of gold. For those who have fallen into it there is only *one* salvation: they must be conducted to the place from which the magic sword borrows its powers."

Now they both thought again about how the hand, the tablet of worlds and times, had also disappeared along with the king and his family. And they thought of how the storm wind had blown away the roads to the places at which the powers renew themselves, and the hand was not there and the king was not present to make known the new roads. And the anguish overwhelmed them more strongly than ever before.

Then the master requested respite and delay for the beleaguered land, which had moved his heart to pity, and the hero granted it. The two agreed on signals by which they would give each other information if something should happen which the one might want to let the other know. Then they parted and the master went his way.

Meanwhile, in order to avert the danger, the people in the country of wealth had decided to employ the respite granted to them to dispatch messengers to that country whose wealth was so infinite that all its inhabitants were esteemed as gods by them. The messengers set forth on their conveyances, but departed by mistake from the right road and lost their way.

While they strayed about in the world searching, they met one day a man who bore in his hands a golden staff completely covered with sparkling stones from which proceeded rays as from a constellation. His hat was encircled with strings of pearls that seemed to assemble in themselves the treasures of all the seas. All the wealth of their gods taken together was like child's play compared with the immeasurable value of the jewels that the stranger bore on himself. At this sight they sank down with faces in the dust and stammered words of adoration; for what could this signify to them but the presence of the god over all gods? But in reality he was the king's treasurer, who at the time when the storm wind had altered the face of the earth had hidden the treasures of his master and since then had guarded them. He bid them rise, and when they asked him anxiously who he was, he gave them this information. Then they implored him to show them the treasures of the king. He led them into the mountain cavern where the vast treasures lay arranged side by side.

When the messengers saw the treasures, they said to one another, "Why then should we still search for those gods? Let us ask this man to go with us, for surely he is mightier than all gods whom we know." They put the request to him, and he was ready to accompany them. He bid them take the treasure and load it on their carts. "But be very careful," he warned them, "not to desire these things in the manner of money, for when one belong to own them and wants to misuse as idle possession the noble blessing that was created to produce joy and to be the adornment of life, they fall to dust before his greedy eyes." The messengers heard this with astonishment, and it was a long time before they had grasped the meaning of the words. Then they loaded themselves with the treasures and set out with them on the way home. During the whole trip they regarded the riches spread out on the wagon only furtively, with shy and anxious glances.

In the country of wealth they were received with delirious jubilation, for now its inhabitants imagined themselves to be safe from the hero since they concealed the god of all gods within their walls. The treasurer, who had recognized the delusion of the country, promulgated laws to guide them; he forbade the worship of the gods, the sacrifice and the abasement of those without possessions. But whatever he undertook and however he exhorted the people, he did not succeed. Since they spoke to him incessantly of the hero, however, and begged him to liberate them from the danger, he went out into the camp and had himself conducted to the commander. Soon they recognized each other with great joy. After a while the hero began to speak and tell of all things that had taken place and also of what the master of prayer had told him. Then they spoke of the country of wealth, and the hero made known to his friend the one way of liberation. Then the treasurer asked him for new respite, and he granted it. They too settled on signals for messages; then they separated.

The treasurer returned to the country of wealth and said to the people, "Take my advice as to the only way in which you can stand steadfast before the hero! In the far distance, at the end of forgotten paths, there lies in twilight magic the place from which the sword of the hero takes its mysterious strength. This place we must seek; there you will become free." This pleased the people well, and they entreated their much-praised gods, the richest men of the land, that these gods themselves should accompany the treasurer. But the treasurer let the hero know his intention, and in the gray of the next morning the hero came to him disguised and joined him. To the master of prayer, too, they sent report. He too came in order to accompany them, greeted the new-found comrade with radiant joy, and now they went forth with the messengers of the foolish country. But since the earth with all its roads had been altered at the time of the storm wind, they decided to travel from kingdom to kingdom until they came to the right place.

After many days of journey, they saw before them the far-extended frontier wall of a country. They stopped a man and asked him what country this was.

"When the great tempest visited the earth and mixed up all its essences," he replied, "the bands of men fell into discord and quarreled with one another over the meaning of life. Each band went its way, to be a people for itself and to select a king according to its views. And we who had recognized that only wisdom is the goal and ground of all permanency, we too did the same and traveled over the surfaces of the earth to seek the wise man who should be our lord. Thus we came on one who sat there with head thrown back and gazed at the stars. 'Are you,' we asked him, 'the wise man who knows the world so well that no dark corner can escape his eyes and no path can lose itself before his searchings?' 'I know the life of the stars,' he answered, 'and so I know the world.' But we spoke further, 'And when the tremor comes over the stars on the day of transformation and dashes them to pieces, what do you know then?' Then he was silent and gave us no answer. And farther on we came on one who lay on the strand and gazed into the sea, and we put to him our question. 'I

137

know the life of the sea,' he said, 'and so I know the world.' Then we asked him, 'And when the sun has drunk up the sea on the day of the turning, what do you know then?' Thereupon he too became silent, and we went further. Thus we met many wise men engrossed in their gazing, and each type of wisdom shattered on our question. Once, however, we caught sight on our way of an old man who sat on a stone, and his eyes were wide open, but not directed in front of him toward any object or being in space; rather, it was a gazing that was enclosed in itself. 'Are you,' we asked him, 'the wise man who knows the world?' Then he looked at us and said, 'I know my soul. It is the firmament that no one can break in pieces. It is the sea that no one can swallow up.' We bowed before him and asked him to be our prince. He went with us, and we took possession of this land.''

Then the master and his people knew that that wise man must be the lost counselor of the king. They had themselves announced to him, he came to meet them and welcomed them with joy, and they discussed with him all the things that had happened and should happen. When they told him of the country of wealth, he said to the master, "It is true that those deluded by gold are to be healed through the road that leads to the place of the sword. But first you must lead them out beyond this place until you come to a dark mountain. If you walk around it with watchful eyes, you will notice a narrow crevice just wide enough for a man to enter through it. Above this door you will see gigantic birds resting or moving in the air, and thereby you may know the right place. The door leads to a cavern. In this cavern is a kitchen in which, from the beginning, the true food of the human race has been prepared in brazen kettles. Fire you will not perceive: it is drawn upward to this place in deep, invisible paths from the fire-mountains of the earth; the birds in the air fan it with their wheeling or soften it, as is needed. The food that the fire cooks is that which delivers one from madness. Yet know, only he who of his own will sets foot on this place will be healed by it."

These were hard words for the master, and he and the wise man exhorted the rich men to awaken their wills. The wise man spoke with great clarity of the futility of money, which is only an empty medium of exchange and has no value and no worth in itself; it receives value and worth only from the useful and beautiful things that it brings together or bears apart. And the master spoke with holy fervor of how all possession of things is vain and transitory, while only the soul that renounces all will to have, possesses

139

true life. They listened to these words attentively, as at earlier times, but as if they were a message in a foreign language out of whose darkness only here and there a comprehensible word sounded forth; but their wills were not moved. Then the master was deeply troubled, and he was close to turning back.

But the wise man said, "Do not let it vex you. I know the day is not distant when the madness will be lifted from the earth like a nightmare at dawn. If to us, too, the way is not known and we can thus barely seek it, as a blind man gropes his way, nonetheless, do not let it annoy you to go farther, and the way will be given to you. And let me, too, go with you. But know that from the storm I have saved the hand, the tablet of the worlds, and I have covered it, and never have I desired to look at it; for this is fitting only for the king to whom alone is given the power to read it. It too I shall take with me that it may remain in my possession." Then they marched away from there together.

After a time they came again to a country, and again they questioned a man whom they met at the wall.

"When the confusion drove men apart from one another, I and my people were those to whom the word appeared to be precious and significant beyond all else. We wandered from place to place in order to seek the master of the word who should be our king. Thus we came to a market place where stood on the platform a man who spoke to the crowd, and his word seemed to lie on the naked heart like the touch of a hand. And we said to one another, 'Now they will go hither like a great wave and do his will!' But when he had finished, the people left him unhurriedly and went about their business as before, and his word barely hovered still above their heads. Another time we came to a garden where many youths sat in a circle around a man; he taught them and explained to them the things of heaven and of earth, and his word was like a stream of fire. And we said to one another, 'Now his word will penetrate into them and enkindle the truth in them.' But when he had finished, one put a question to another, and he answered according to the answer of the master; for the word had died in their spirit and lay there like heavy slag. And so it befell us yet many times.

"But one morning we came to a forest clearing where a man leaned on a tree and sang to himself in a singular manner; for he sang and sang, and then he became silent and the trees rustled to him a sister song, and while he remained silent great voices came forth from the rocks; and again he began, and then

141

the things were silent and listened, but as he ceased, a bird was heard and soon a chorus of birds, and a brook answered their silence and sang. Thus the song of the man was around him and lived in all places and yet was always different and new, for each of the things sang it in its own good way. The things and beings relayed the song; the air itself became a singing mouth and bore the melody into the worlds. We too were seized by the desire to sing it; it came to our lips, and our hearts were full of it. It was still in us as we bowed before him and asked him to come with us as our prince."

Then the master of prayer and his friends knew that this could be no other than the singer of the king. They asked to be taken to him and greeted him with joy. When he had discovered the purpose of their journey, he too went with them.

After a long trip they came together to the border of a country, and again they questioned one of its dwellers.

"We are the ones," he said, "to whom in those days of disputing it became clearer than ever that nothing is like beauty, which perseveres in the whirl-wind and survives all assault unchanged. So we decided to wander through the earth and seek a being of beauty in order to place the mastery over us in his hands. But the ages went by and still we strayed about without a lord. For everywhere the peace of the countenance was distorted by greed and the eyes troubled by senseless images. So we were already close to despairing of our goal when, in a deserted wilderness, we met with a strange woman. She sat alone in the wilderness, and her face was white and motionless. Never had we beheld such beauty and never such anguish, for it possessed her without destroying her beauty. We kneeled before the woman and expressed our wish that she might become our sovereign. Three times we had to state our request before she heard us. At the third time she inclined her head. And although she remained immutably imprisoned in her pain, she became our gracious mistress."

Thus the king's daughter was found, and she too went away with her father's people; for in her, as in them, there grew hope and anticipation.

They continued for a while, then came to a country that lay in silence, and only with difficulty could they obtain information from one of the inhabitants.

"This is the land of death," he said, "and we who live here live under the wings of death. For when the other men would not recognize his power, we detached ourselves from them and marched forth to seek his viceroy on earth. For a long time we were not privileged to find him. Still once at the end of a grotto we met a woman with white hair who stood there rigid, and we saw that she stood under the spell of death. From her eyes bloody tears fell upon the barren ground, for they had destroyed all life, blade and bud. We took her upon our royal chariot, brought her here, and founded our kingdom."

The master and his friends had themselves led before the queen and bowed over her hands, and the king's daughter put her arms about her neck; still she did not awaken out of her stiffness. But when the master spoke of the way, then she stirred, and when he told of how the goal had become clearer for them from path to path, then she arose to accompany them.

They came together to a country where one to whom they turned with their question told them, "We are the servants of honor. When we separated ourselves from the rest of the world, we wanted to make one who was a son and chosen one of honor our king. We searched for one who persisted in so pure and honest a sense of the right that he would be worthy to be our ruler. But there was no one who approached such in our eyes. Until the stars guided us to our king. He sat on a hill, his crown lay beside him, but his head was surrounded by a mysterious luster. His glance penetrated into future spheres. All that was around him silently paid homage to him. Bowed to the earth we honored the ground at his feet, and we elevated him over us as our prince."

On the threshold of the palace the king met his followers, and all numbness melted before his greeting. The grace of the moment took fire in all hearts. But now, too, the image of the lost child did not vanish from them. Then the king spoke, "The time is fulfilled. the ways are opened, error is transformed into knowledge, want into abundance. Let us march forth to the country of the child." They went thither with the king and came, by the road that he indicated to them, into a land that was the country of peace, and they were received with joy by the people of the land. These were the people that in the days of contention had vowed themselves to joy and had gone into the world to choose the most joyful for their king.

Yet nowhere did they find a laughter in which lived the soul; each was broken and bitter. Thus they sought a long while. But one day they encountered running on a highway a child that ran alone and laughing, its shining locks fluttering about it and its firm little arms outstretched in the morning wind. It laughed at stones, trees and animals as if they were telling it something. Then the wandering people said to one another, "Where on earth is there a joy like this? All men laugh over some happenings, and their laughter runs aground on other happenings. But this child laughs at life as if it bore in secure spirit all that will happen, and its joy nourishes itself on the gleam of future things." They chose the child as their ruler.

This they now reported to the king and his followers. While they still spoke, the child came running up to them laughing and stretched out its arms to all of them.

This was the hour of joy. The foolish gods from the country of wealth stood there and gaped and could not in the least comprehend what happiness had come over their companions since they had still received nothing of gold or of the value of gold.

Then they too were remembered. The road to the place of the cavern in which the healing food was prepared was now open, for the hand, the tablet of the worlds, was uncovered, and the king again read in it as before. But the king confirmed the word of the wise man: only he who set foot in the place of his own would become cured by it. And so all the comrades exhorted the men from the country of wealth to awaken their wills. Yet none of their words were able to penetrate the deaf hearts. But it now happened that some of the gold coins that the rich men carried with them fell from them to the ground. The child fixed its eyes upon them; the glittering disks pleased it; it picked them up, threw them in the air, and laughed. Then the seed of laughter fell into the deaf hearts and sprouted in them. The men said to one another, "How does it happen that our souls are fixed on these shining things?" A great anxiety for their inner life crept over them; suddenly it seemed to them without meaning. But still they could not extricate themselves. They called to the master of prayer with loud and imploring voices, "Help us out!"

Then the master took with him the people from the possessed land, trod with them the road that led into the cavern, and gave them of the food to eat. Only now did the whole shame of money grow in them. They cast from them all the gold that they were carrying with them as something unspeakably shameful, and so great was their shame that they wanted with their hands to dig a hole for themselves in the earth, on the place where they were standing, in order to hide themselves. But the master raised them up by his encouragement. He bid them take the food and bring it into their country that all could taste it and be healed. So it happened, and shame was enkindled

**147**

in the country of wealth. Even the insignificant people who had been called animals were ashamed that up till now they had been so small in their own eyes only because they possessed no money.

But since the ways were open, each of the king's followers went to his place to renew his strength. And when this had happened and they again had power over the souls of the human race, the king sent them out into all countries, to heal all madness, to enlighten all illusion, and to disentangle all bewilderment and perplexity. The peoples became purified; all turned to the true meaning of life and dedicated themselves to God.

# THE
# SEVEN BEGGARS

It happened in olden times that a country was visited by the curse of war. While the men able to bear arms went out to meet the enemy, the enemy invaded the land from the rear, found the wives and children defenseless, seized their goods and forced them to flee. Pursued thus by need and fright, the banished ones hurried through the woods. In the haste and confusion it happened that two mothers each lost one of her children. They were a little boy and a little girl who had played together and now were united in their destitution. After they had played for half a day further and had amused themselves with moss and stones, hunger began to torment them; they clasped each other's hands and walked weeping ever deeper into the forest. At last they came to a path. When they had followed it for a while, they met a beggar who had a full pouch hanging at his side. They ran to him, clung and pressed close to him, and begged him not to leave them alone. He handed them bread and food and let them fill themselves; but then he bid them continue of good cheer and of good courage, for he could not accompany them. While he spoke thus, the children looked him in the face and perceived that he was blind; they were greatly astonished at how he could go hence so sure of his way. But the blind man left them and blessed them with the words, "May you be as I am."

The children wandered farther. Night set in upon them; they found a hollow tree and laid themselves in it to rest. When they awoke in the morning, they arose and went farther. After a while they again felt the need of nourishment, and they began to cry. Then they again met a beggar on their way, and they pleaded with him, as they had pleaded with the blind man the day before. He made signs to them that he was deaf and could not hear them, but he saw that they were hungry and forlorn and he gave them food and drink. As he turned, he motioned to them to follow him. He directed them to go further on their way and not to despair; and he too blessed them with the words, "May you be as I am." The following day, as hunger again began to torture them, they once more met a beggar to whom they complained of their distress. He listened to them and answered, but they could not understand him, for he had a thick tongue and stuttered. He handed them food and drink and comforted them, but would not take them with him. He too departed with the same good wish as the earlier ones. On the fourth day they found a beggar with a crooked neck, on the fifth a hunchback, on the sixth a man with crippled hands, and on the seventh a man with lame feet. Each bestowed on them nourishment and encouragement and blessed them in the same manner.

On the eighth day they left the great forest and saw lying before them in the valley, friendly and sparkling, a village. They entered the first house and asked for bread, and they were given it copiously. Thus they went from door to door, and when they left the village, had more than their hands could hold. They then resolved that from that time on they would never separate from each other and that they would both live on the kindness of men. They sewed themselves large pouches in order to hold in them the gifts that they would receive. Thus they roamed through the land; they were seen at every market place in the band of beggars, and they joined themselves to every festival and every wedding. Soon the pretty young figures won the love of their comrades

151

as, tender and simple, they sat thus on the threshold between the weather-beaten old men with the plate in their little hands. Every beggar in the land knew the lost children and protected them as if they were his own blood when he met them.

Thus the time passed, and the children grew up. Once a year in the capital city of the country there was a great market at which many men from all regions gathered. There were many kinds of games and merriment there, all hands were gentle and open, gifts flowed in abundance to the beggars, none of whom were absent, and they too were jolly and in good spirits. They looked joyfully at the two young people in their midst, and in the gay mood of the festival the idea struck them of marrying to each other the two who from childhood on had always remained together. The lad and the maiden were quite willing, and there was only one problem: how to prepare the place of the wedding and the wedding dinner. Yet for that too counsel was soon found. One of the beggars proposed that they should wait until the celebration of the king's birthday; then there would be food and drink aplenty for the beggar folk; all that they should receive of roasts, cakes, and wine they should collect and furnish the wedding with it. So it happened.

On the evening before the holiday, however, the beggars had decorated a cavern in front of the city with green sprigs and wild flowers, had shoved together huge stones for a table and prepared a wedding canopy out of flowering bushes. The beggars came to the wedding and brought their gifts. But in the midst of their happiness the bridal pair recalled the day when, as little children, they had been lost in the forest and the blind beggar had kindheartedly stilled their hunger and comforted them. Their hearts were filled with longing to see the old man again. While they sat and reflected on their yearning, a shadow fell on the entrance of the cave and in the entrance there appeared a stooped figure, dark against the light of heaven.

A voice said, "See, here I am," and they recognized the first beggar who had met them in the forest. "I have come," he said further, "in order to offer to you my gift for the wedding. Once, when you were children, I blessed you with the wish that you might be as I am. Today I present to you as an accomplished fact that you shall have a life like mine. You imagine that I am blind. But I am not blind. Rather all earthly time does not touch me and does not concern me, even for the twinkling of an eye. I am very old and still quite young, and I have not yet begun to live.

And that is not of my own choosing, but the great eagle has revealed and imparted it to me. This is what took place:

"It happened once that a band of men undertook a trip on the ocean on well-equipped ships. But then they sailed into a great storm and they were overcome by it, managing to save nothing except their lives and even doing this only through their good fortune in reaching an island which had unexpectedly appeared to them while they were swimming. As they explored the tiny isle, they saw a tower that rose in the center. They entered it and met with no living being, but, for all that, found everything that served the necessities of life. When evening came on, they had conquered the fatigue of their bodies through a short sleep and gathered around a cheerful light. One among them came up with the proposal that they should tell stories. Each should bring forward the oldest event that he recalled and the first source of his memory. But since there were gray-haired men as well as youths, they rendered the honor to the oldest and asked him to narrate first.

"He was a man as old as the seas who spoke with a voice that came out of the distance, 'What shall I tell you? I remember the day when one broke the apple from the branch.' Then the next oldest arose

154

and said, 'But I still think of the time when the light burned.' And the third, who was still younger, cried, 'I can recall the day when the fruit began to form.' 'But my thoughts,' joined in the fourth, 'reach unto the hour when the seed fell into the flower-cup!' 'And to me is still present,' said a fifth, 'how the flavor of the fruit entered into the seed.' 'And to me,' interjected the sixth, 'how the fragrance of the fruit entered into the seed.' 'And I still have within me,' spoke the seventh, 'how the shape of the fruit joined with the bud.' But I, who at that time was still a boy," spoke the blind beggar further, "was also with them. And I said to them, 'I recollect all these occurrences and I recollect nothing at all.' They were all greatly astonished that the youngest had the earliest memory and the child knew of the most ancient happening.

"Then came the great eagle, rapped on the tower, and bade them all step outside in the order of their ages: the boy he bade go before all, for he was really the oldest in memory, and the oldest he led out last, for he was really the youngest. And the great eagle spoke, 'Can you remember how you were detached from the body of your mother, or how you grew in your mother's body? Can you recollect the hour when the seed fell into your mother's womb? Can you recall your spirit before it entered into the seed, or your soul, or your life before it entered into the seed? This lad is above you all, for there still stirs within his inward mind the shadow of the primordial beginning, and the breath of the great night has not withdrawn from him. Thus he stands on the abyss of eternity as on native ground.'

"And the great eagle spoke further to them, 'The ships on which you came have been dashed to pieces; but they will be rebuilt and will go back.' To me, however, he said—and his voice was like the voice of a brother—'You come with me and be with me wherever you go, for you are like me. You are old and quite young, and have not yet begun to live, and so am I, old and quite young, and the ages of ages are before me. And so you can remain.' That is what the great eagle said to me. And this, you children, I present to you today as a wedding gift, that you may be like me." With these words of the blind beggar a rush of great joy went through the cave, but the hearts of the bridegroom and the bride stood still.

On the second day of the wedding the bridal pair sat silently in the ranks of the merry and recalled, full of sadness, the second beggar, the deaf man who had fed them when they had strayed about in the great forest. While they were wishing for him, they saw him standing before them without their having noticed his coming.

"Here I am since you desire me," he addressed them, "and I have come that you may possess through me what I once spoke over you as a blessing—that you should be like me. You believe that I am deaf. I am not deaf. My ear is only shut to the great cry of need that ascends from the world. For the voice of every creature is born out of need. But all their calling cannot reach me, and my heart is not seized by the anxiety of creation. And with the bread that I eat and the water that I drink, I live a good life without want and greed. To this I have a testimony from the mouths of the people who live in the kingdom of plenty. A group of them once gathered, and they praised highly and with great words the glorious life that they lived in their homes where everything prospers in abundance. Then I, who was present, said, 'Your life is futile and a wretched game compared with mine.' They eyed my gray costume and my beggar's pouch and laughed over me as over a fool.

"But I spoke to them, 'Now then, we shall test whose life is the better. I know a country that was once a great, wonderful garden where thrived the most precious fruits of the earth in unheard-of luxuriousness, fruits whose appearance, fragrance, and enjoyment so delighted and refreshed all the senses of the inhabitants that it seemed to them that never and nowhere could the bliss of their life be surpassed. Over all their province a gardener was set who seeded and planted with wisdom and fostered the beauty and fruitfulness of the country each year anew. But it happened one night that the gardener disappeared, and no one knew where he was. Then from year to year the blessing passed from the garden; the rank shoots grew rampant and in unchecked abundance, the wilderness overran the land, and from one harvest to the next the yield declined.

" 'Nonetheless, the inhabitants would have been able to nourish themselves from the rich young offshoots if another misfortune had not overtaken them. A cruel foreign king came marching with his band and took possession of the country. He was not able to ravish their garden, as in his imperturbable impetus to destruction he certainly would have liked to do; so he decided to disturb the purity of the senses of its inhabitants, and while he hastened onward in his march of conquest, he left behind the three most unbridled and vicious bands of his vassals. These lived from then on among the people of the country, infected them with their depravity and brought corruption, calumny, and fornication among them. Then the people's senses, once nourished from the free innocence of the garden, became clouded; their eyes saw only confusion and darkness; their mouths tasted only bitter tastes, and their nostrils smelled only the stench of putrefaction. As a result, they were disgusted by the food that the garden offered; its fragrances bewildered them and its appearance filled them with aversion. Now go hence, you sons of luxury, and help them out of the fullness of your good life.'

"Then the people got ready and went with me into the country of the garden. But when they had reached it, the abomination of corruption was so great that the sight of it bewildered the senses of the rich people themselves and the taste of their mouths became loathsome to them. Then I spoke to them, 'Now you have become well aware that all of your good life cannot be of help in this.' I assembled the people of the garden, offered them the bread and the water that I carried in my pouch, and divided it among all of them. And lo, the goodness of my life conquered them; they tasted in my bread and in my water all the pleasing odors and pleasant tastes of all the food of the world. Their senses again attained clarity and purity. They abhorred their perverted life, roused themselves, and drove the vassals of the cruel king out of the land. Soon the vanished gardener stood in their midst, and each saw and felt the old blessing return. But the people from the kingdom of plenty beheld how they had been redeemed through me and recognized the power and fullness of my good life. Now to you, you children, the wedding gift that I present today is that you may be like me." When the deaf beggar had spoken this, the ringing jubilation again went through the cavern, and the second day of the festival passed in radiant joy.

When the third morning dawned, the bridal pair was again overcome by anxiety, and there grew overpoweringly in them the longing for the third beggar, the stammerer who had fed and blessed them in the forest. As they began to talk of him, "Could one but know where he stays, to call him and invite him!," he stood before them as if he had emerged from the heart of the earth, took them in his arms and spoke in a clear and audible voice:

"Once I blessed you with the wish that you might be like me; today my blessing shall descend upon you and be revealed to you. You think that my only speech is stuttering, but this is not so. Rather, the utterances of a world not dedicated to God, utterances that are only unworthy fragments of the true

160

word, sound like shards in my mouth. Great power of speech has been bestowed on me, and the noblest song has been allotted to me as the master of singers; there is no creature that does not listen to me until my tone trembles through his soul like the tone of the purest bell through the clear atmosphere. And in the song is a wisdom that is beyond all the wisdom of the world.

"This is assured me from the mouth of the powerful man who is called the man of true grace. For I go over the earth and collect all good deeds and all works of grace and bring them to him. And out of the good deeds and the works of grace, time is born and renews itself in the eternal stream. For time is no secure thing and no being from all eternity; it is something that is created, and it is created out of the deeds of the souls. I will tell you the saying of all sayings which is the profoundest and most primal of all truths:

"At the final abyss of space stands a mountain on which lies a rock and from the rock flows a fountain. But know that each thing in the world has a heart. And that mountain with the rock and the fountain stands on the one rim of space where the final abyss begins, and the heart of the world stands on the other rim of space, where the final abyss ends. And the

161

heart of the world stands there opposite the fountain, and it looks out toward it over the distance of space, and it longs for the fountain with great yearning. But if in its distress it becomes weakened and wants to rest for awhile and breathe deeply again, a great bird comes and spreads its wings over it, and then it rests for a while in its shadow. After the rest, it rouses itself to go to the fountain. But as soon as it moves toward it, the mountain vanishes from its sight. And if it should lose sight of the fountain entirely, then it must perish, for its life depends on the fountain. And along with the heart the world must perish, for its life and the life of each thing depends on the heart, and only through it do they continue to exist. But as soon as the sight of the mountain vanishes from the heart, the desire to behold the fountain becomes more powerful than the drive to reach it, and the heart returns to its place.

"But duration is not given to the fountain, for it is beyond time and can obtain no temporal life of itself. And so it must remain eternally concealed in the timeless and cannot become manifest to the heart. But it receives from the heart a temporal life. For the heart presents it with A Day; it offers it to it as a gift, and thus the fountain endures. And when the day declines and issues into the evening, then they speak to each other the words of parting and the final blessing. And the heart stands in great dread and will expire, for it has nothing more to give than A Day, and the anxiety is upon it that the fountain will be carried away from it beyond the limits of time.

"But the man of true grace watches with knowing eyes over heart and fountain. And when the evening expands into night, he presents to the heart a new day, and the heart presents the day to the fountain. But know, the time that the man of grace bestows he has from my hand. For I go over the earth and gather all good deeds and all works of grace. Then I speak over them the words of the great unification, and they become a melody, and this I bring to the man of true grace, and he creates out of it time. For time is born of melody and melody of grace. And so from the songs the days flow forth and come to the heart and from the heart to the fountain, and thus the world continues and endures in its dread. But eternal word and song fill my soul. And this I present today to you, you children, as a wedding gift, that you may be like me." Silently, with forehead bowed, the two received the speech of the beggar. The third day passed from them silently, but inwardly full of blessed song.

On the fourth day a longing came over them for

the beggar with the crooked neck who had once
showed so much kindness to them. And again, summoned by their yearning, he unexpectedly stood before them and said, "I have come here to renew my
blessing of the forest where you were children. You
think, do you not, that I have a twisted neck and am
not able to look you in the eye with a straight face?
I have an upright neck like you. But I turn my face
away from the vanities of men and will not mix my
breath with their breath. My neck and my chest are
so well built, however, that I can produce out of my
throat all the voices of creatures which are not lan-
guages, and there is no sound so strange that I cannot
portray it in its manner.

"That has been confirmed for me by the people in
the country of music. There is a country where the
melodies peal through the streets a thousandfold and
yet related, and there even the babbling of children
is song. One time the masters of that country told each
other tales of the voices dwelling in them that wanted
to go forth into outer life. Then I, who was with
them, addressed them and said, 'But my voice par-
takes of all the sounds that never reach you. For
from the primordial beginning all creatures to whom
the word has not been given long for my coming,
which lifts to tone what lies mute in their hearts. If

164

you wish to measure yourselves against me, come on! There are two human kingdoms that are a thousand miles distant from each other. When the night comes, then the men of those kingdoms find no sleep, but wander about, clasping their temples with weary hands and lamenting a bitter lament. Each creature sighs, and even from the stones there ascends a fixed wail. Come now, you masters, help those kingdoms conquer the lament of the voices!'

"Then they demanded that I lead them to one of the kingdoms, and I led them there. It was evening when we came to the border of that kingdom. As soon as we were at the border, their voices united with the great chorus of laments that ascended from the land. Then I said to them, 'You see now how your might succumbs and is helplessly dragged along by a greater. I will tell you what is the matter here. There are two birds, a little husband and a little wife, who are the only pair of their kind. One day it came to pass that they became separated from each other and could not find each other again. Then they became anxious and while they imagined they were getting nearer each other in their seeking, they flew ever farther apart and fluttered and called until at last they sank down exhausted and never hoped to find each other again. Each came to rest in the branches of the nearest tree. It happened that the one was in one, and the other in the other, of the two kingdoms, and the thousand miles lay between them. There they now lament the lament of their yearning, each from his place in the distance. By day all the birds from the forest round about come to each of the two, comfort it with a thousand twittering and cooing calls and encourage it to feel that it will again find its mate; and so the heart of each remains silent by day, although it trembles and is full of grief. But when evening comes and the bands have flown away and the noises are hushed, then each again feels how it is alone in the world and begins its lament. The lament resounds and reverberates into the distance, and none who hears it can withstand it; it compels all to join in and surges through the land like a powerful flood. When the lament thus surges through the land, the inner woe of every being is in it, for each being's most secret pain has entered into it. Thus the two kingdoms live in lamentation night after night.'

"Then the masters said to me, 'Come then, and you, can you help them?' 'I certainly can do so,' I replied. 'For since the voices of all beings are living in me and each voice has entrusted to me its song, I am aware of the suffering of all things.' I led the masters away in order to free them from the lament and returned with them into their country, which lay between the two kingdoms. And since I am able not only to produce the voices of all things, but can also make them resound at the place that I choose, I created in my throat the voice of the little husband and sent it to the little wife, and I created the voice of the little wife and sent it to the little husband. So the two birds heard each other in my voice; they trembled and sat still upon their twigs and for a while could not move. But then they flew up and toward the call and found each other at the place where I sat with the masters. Thus their lament was stilled. But to you, you children, the wedding gift I present you this day is that you may be like me." Then the great compassion and the helping strength entered into the hearts of the two.

On the fifth day the memory of the fifth beggar, the hunchback, troubled their joy, and they yearned for him that he might take part in their holiday. There he stood already before them, grasped their hands and said, "Here I have come to your wedding to change my own blessing into a present. I wished over your childhood that you might be like me. It seems to you that I am hunchbacked; that is an illusion and arises from the fact that I bear the burdens of the world on my back. But my back is straight and strong, and it has the gift of the small that conquers the great. For

I bear on my back all burdens of the world: anxiety, misery, and weariness—I take all of them on my shoulders and bear them. Once the wise men assembled and spoke about who really has the gift of the small that conquers the great. One said, 'My brain is the small that conquers the great, for in my brain I carry the necessities of thousands upon thousands of men who depend on me and out of my brain I feed them and give to each his portion.' Then they laughed at him and shook their heads. And another spoke, 'My word is the small that conquers the great. For I have been appointed by my king to receive all praises and all requests and all thanks and bring them before him in my word. And my word raises them all and speaks to them.' Then they again shook their heads, and a third said, 'My silence is the small that conquers the great. For everywhere adversaries rise against me, they contend with me and pelt me with their words to dishonor me. I am silent toward them, and that is my answer to all.' Then they again shook their heads, and a fourth spoke, 'My seeing is the small that conquers the great. For I grasp with my eyes the round dance of the world. Seeing, I lead the great blind man, the world—a tiny man leading the monster. Altogether subject to it, yet I lead it with my eyes that grasp its round dance."

168

Then they were silent and looked at him who had spoken.

"But I said to them, 'This man here is the greatest of you, but I am superior to him, and I have the gift of the small that conquers the great. For I bear on my back all the burdens of the world. I will disclose to you a certain matter. It is known to you that each animal knows a shadow in which alone it can rest, and each bird knows a bough on which alone it can rest. But do you also know that there is a tree whose shadow all the beasts of the field and whose boughs all the birds of heaven select for a resting place?' Then they answered, 'We do, indeed, know it from our forefathers, and we know that all the happiness of life is nothing compared with the great happiness of staying by that tree, for all beings are brothers and sisters there and play with one another. But we have no information as to how we can get to the tree, for some say that one must go east, and some think that one must take the path to the west, and we are unable to discover the path.'

"Then I said to them, 'Why do you inquire by what way you can reach the tree? Inquire, first of all, who and what and of what nature are the men who can reach the tree. For this is not destined for every one; it is for none save him who has the gift of the tree. But the tree has three roots from which comes its gift; the one root is called faith, the other root is called fidelity, the third root is called humility, and truth is the trunk of the tree; and only he who has all these can reach the tree.' Then they accepted my words, and because not all had those gifts, they decided to wait until all should be worthy. He who lacked perfection strove and wrestled to acquire it. But in the moment when all were at last allotted the gifts in the same degree, they also all suddenly saw the way illumined. They prepared themselves and set out, and I went with them.

"We went a long time until we caught sight of the tree from the distance. They looked at it and there stood the tree on no place; it stood there and yet had no place, and no space was around it, and it was separated from all space. And they despaired of reaching it. But I said to them, 'I can bring you to the tree. For it stands beyond space; and because I bear all the burdens of the world in the manner of the smallest that conquers the greatest, I have overcome the space in me and destroyed its traces in my soul; and there where I am its dominion is at an end and it is only One Step from there to where space is not. So I shall now bring you to the tree.' And I did so. But you, you children, be allotted my power to bear, and this

I present to you today as a wedding gift that you may be like me."

Thus grew from day to day the fullness of the miraculous gifts and the joy. But on the sixth day both again sat in longing and recalled the beggar with the crippled hands, and they fervently wished him there. And again he too stood before them, greeted them, and said, "My former blessing shall now become true for you. You imagine that my hands are disabled and that I cannot move them. But in reality, I am only unable to employ them for any work that does not liberate the fettered and deliver the captive. My hands are strong and work in the depths and in the distances. Once the strong men assembled, and each praised the strength of his hands. One said, 'I can grasp an arrow in its flight and send it home to its starting point, and the arrow that has found its goal I am able to check so that its deed comes to nought.' Then I asked him, 'Over which arrow is such might given to you? For there are ten kinds of arrows, dipped in ten different kinds of poison.' He answered, such and such a kind of arrow was subject to his strength. 'Then you will not heal the king's daughter,' I said to him. 'For you will not draw the ten arrows out of her heart.'

"Now another spoke, 'I am able to open the prisons

with my hands, and their gates spring open when my finger touches them.' 'Which prison do you open?,' I then asked him. 'For there are ten kinds of prisons, and the hinges of their gates are of ten different forms.' He answered that such and such a kind could not withstand him. 'Then you will not heal the king's daughter,' I said to him. 'For you cannot enter freely over the ten walls of water that surround her castle. For only he who creates the whole freedom moves freely.' A third said, 'I can distribute wisdom with my hands, and I bestow wisdom on each on whom I lay my hands.' Then I asked him, 'Which wisdom is it that you dispense? For there are ten kinds of wisdom, and each gives only a piece of the true being. He answered that he possessed such and such kind of wisdom in abundance. 'Then you will not heal the king's daughter,' I said to him. 'For you cannot recognize her ten afflictions. For only he who dispenses the whole wisdom recognizes the hidden.' A fourth boasted of himself, 'I can grasp with my hands the wing of the storm wind and direct it.' Then I asked him, 'Which storm wind do you command? For there are ten storm winds, and each sings its song, and he teaches it to you if you are his master.' He could compel such and such a storm wind, he answered. 'Then you will not heal the king's daughter,' I said to him. 'For you cannot sing before her the ten songs that are her salvation. And the songs are in the might of the storms.'

"But they asked me, 'And what can you do, you who judge us?' 'I can do all that you can do,' I spoke, 'and I can do all that you cannot do. I have opened the prisons of the earth, both these and those, and I can walk freely on the waves. I have power over all missiles, and from all wounds I draw forth the poisoned arrows and nullify their effects. I have dispensed all the treasures of wisdom out of my fullness, and the strength is given me to fathom all that is secret. I have hitched the storm winds to my wagon, and in their soughing I learned their melodies. And I can heal the king's daughter.

" 'But know, once a prince desired a king's daughter; he employed artifices to catch her, and he succeeded in getting her in his hand. But a short time thereafter the prince dreamed that she stood above his bed, and her hands were placed around his throat and strangled him. Then he awoke, but the dream had pierced his heart. He summoned the interpreters, and they explained to him that it would happen according to the happenings of the dream, that he must come to die through the king's daughter. Then the prince's soul knew not what to do; for it was painful to him to kill the king's daughter since she was so beautiful, and it was painful to him to banish her for he could not endure thinking of her as another's, and it was painful to him to leave her near him since he was attached to life and did not want to leave it before he should have grown weary of it.

" 'Meanwhile, his fear began to permeate the glance with which he regarded the king's daughter and the words that he spoke to her. As she saw him go about so dark and distrustful, the love that she had acquired for him was little by little destroyed. At last, she could no longer endure his glance and fled from there. Fleeing, she came to the water castle that stands on the flood behind the ten walls of waves. All this, castle and walls and the place where she stood, all was of water, and no one could step over the threshold, for he would sink into the billows. When the king's daughter stood before the walls, she looked around and saw that the prince was pursuing her with his people, and nowhere was there a way to escape from him. So she stood, turned her face toward the water, and closed her eyes. She heard behind her the tramp of thousands of hoofs, before her the roaring of the great waters, and any sort of existence or any sort of death seemed to her preferable to returning into misery. Then she laid her arms about her neck, threw back her head, and ran into the flood. But the flood bore her, the walls were open, and she ran through the ten gates into the castle.

" 'The king, however, had seen her plunge into the water. He was seized by fury, and he cried to his archers to shoot her. The archers stretched their bows, the arrows whirred, yet they did not reach her. But when she stood at the entrance of the castle, she turned, her eyes opened, and she looked at the prince. Then came the last ten arrows and pierced her heart, and she sank down on the threshold; but the waves bore her into the castle and made a bed for her. The prince and his people followed after her, then sank in the flood. But now I shall go there and heal the king's daughter; for the time is fulfilled, and I hear the command to go forth.' I went to that place and healed the king's daughter. But to you, you children, I present today as a wedding gift the strength of my hands and this, that you may be like me." Then joy ascended anew, and they celebrated their feast with great joy.

*    *    *    *

"The end of this tale, that is, the story of the seventh beggar and the conclusion, we did not have the honor of hearing. And He spoke and said that he might not tell it further. This is a great loss. For we shall not be privileged to hear it until the Messiah comes. May this happen soon, in our days. Amen."

# RABBI NACHMAN'S
# JOURNEY
# TO PALESTINE

# RABBI NACHMAN'S
# JOURNEY
# TO PALESTINE*

In Rabbi Nachman of Bratzlav, the great-grandson
of the Baal-Shem-Tov, the founder of Hasidism,
everything was gathered together and concentrated,
with and also without his knowledge, that the generations of the Diaspora had felt, dreamt and thought
about the land of Israel. He must be seen as the great
heir, who uses his inheritance magnanimously. It is
characteristic of his nature and his mission that he
became, without any literary ambitions of any kind,
simply through oral intercourse with his disciples, the
creator of a literary genre, the symbolical fairy tale,
but that in this new form age-old treasures of mystic
tradition were assimilated and endowed with a su-
preme splendor. He is the best example possible of the

* This chapter by courtesy of East and West Library reprinted
from *Israel and Palestine* by Martin Buber. Translated from the
German by Stanley Goodman.

179

relationship of the Hasidic movement to Palestine: everything flows together in him and everything finds exemplary expression in his life and words. But at the same time we are aware of something else here, something new, that seems to be connected in a strange fashion with our own problems and struggles.

The Hasidic movement, which came to life somewhat suddenly in Eastern European Jewry in the middle of the eighteenth century, must be seen as the last intensive effort in modern history to rejuvenate a religion. To judge merely by the degeneration of the movement that has now been going on for more than a century, it seems to have been a failure; but it has not merely produced an abundance of splendid religious life and of its transfiguration in legend, such as the world has only very seldom seen arise from its midst, but it has also scattered seed in other spheres some of which has already come up and the rest of which will probably develop later on. Some day it will be impossible to see and understand the best of what has arisen and is arising now in the way of new human life in the Jewish settlement of Palestine without connecting it with Hasidism.

The relationship of this movement to the land of Israel cannot be reduced to a formula. It is only possible to do justice to it from the point of view of its relationship to Messianism and this can only be understood in its turn by taking into account the reaction which followed the movement of Sabbatian heaven-storming. Here the Messianic passion burst all bounds, people imagined they saw with their own eyes and grasped with their own hands the consummation of Creation, the renewal of all things, the marriage of heaven and earth. The Law seemed to be abolished in a changed world, and what had formerly been considered sin not merely set free but sanctified. The collapse of the Sabbatian venture signified the danger of spiritual destruction for a Jewry whose soul had been kindled by its fiery breath. The danger was directly perceived when Jakob Frank, the sinister epigone of Sabbatai—one of the most interesting examples of the influence which a man living in unrestrained self-deception is able to exert in times eager for self-deception—swept crowds of Polish Jews into his movement and into chaos. The Baal-Shem rises against this threat of disintegration; he is the antagonist of the fascinating lie. As such both he and his disciples have to try to decontaminate the seriously diseased body of Messianism. The feverish overexcitement of the hour has to give way to a simultaneously enthusiastic and considerate contribution to the cohesion of the times, the place of the unleashing of the instincts is taken by their sublimation (what is right in this concept of modern psychology is already expressed here in the clearest and most emphatic terms), and the daring incarnation phantasies are displaced by the quiet experience of intercourse with the divine in daily life. This naturally also leads to a change in the relationship to Palestine. Without losing the mystical luminosity which adhered to it from Talmudic times and had been powerfully developed in the Kabbala, the land is nevertheless stripped of the web of a slick magic which had entangled it in the period of heaven-storming. It is quite true that contact with the Holy Land is expected to prepare the way for redemption and that the legend bids Baal-Shem-Tov attach the highest possible hopes to a meeting that can only take place there; but at least early, classical Hasidism put an end to the "pressing the end" and the disciples of the founder and their disciples who settle alone or with a whole community of followers in Palestine are obviously thinking not of the unrepeatable miracle but of the continuity of the generations. The mystery has remained, but it has taken up its dwelling in the harsh reality of the tasks of daily life.

It is from here that even the founder's own attitude to Palestine is to be understood. We have little authentic knowledge of it or indeed of his life in general;

but it is clear from the well-known letter to his brother-in-law who had settled there that he considered for a long time traveling to the Holy Land and had not given up the hope even then, about eight years before his death. Hints dropped by disciples of his indicate that he really did begin the journey on one occasion. Why he gave it up is not known. "He was prevented by heaven," the legend says, and the fact that it says so shows that a question to which the storytellers sought to find an answer thrust itself on their attention at this point; in saying which we must note that the telling of this legend, however much apocryphal matter may have become attached to it later on, begins amongst the disciples themselves and in the third generation of Baal-Shem-Tov's own family, which had still known him personally. The various attempts of the legend to answer the question are characteristic. Already in his youth, when he was living with his wife in a hut on the slopes of the Carpathian mountains, dug clay and traveled to the nearest small town to sell it, a band of robbers whose quarrels he was in the habit of settling is said to have offered to lead him to Palestine through caves and subterranean passages; but just as he was about to cross a deep bog with them on the way, the revolving sword of the Cherubs is said to have appeared to him and he had to turn back. At a later date (for it is said that he was accompanied not only by his daughter but also, according to another version, by her sons) he is reported by the legend to have reached Istambul; here he was either warned in a dream and bidden to return, or he embarked with his family and a great storm broke out. At this point the stories part company again. According to one version his daughter falls into the sea from the battered ship, Satan appears and offers him his help but he resists the temptation and decides to return home and immediately all danger is overcome. According to another version, he lands on an island with a disciple where they are taken prisoner, and both are afflicted with a numbness in which they even forgot the words of their prayer; finally the disciple discovers that he still knows the alphabet, he recites it to his master, who repeats it after him "with powerful enthusiasm," and at once liberation comes near and they return home. Similar things take place in other versions. There is an unmistakable tendency throughout the legend to warn against magical intentions in connection with Palestine: so long as the hour of redemption has not arrived, even the chosen are unable to conjure it up. This is a tendency which is abandoned again in later Hasidism, or rather one about which a violent struggle takes place; the Baal-Shem legend is still unmistakably determined by it.

Nearly forty years had passed since the death of Baal-Shem-Tov when his great-grandson made ready to travel to the Holy Land. He was twenty-six at the time.

Here we are not dependent on the legend: his disciple and apostle Nathan recorded the journey step by step in accordance with his own information; the ground we are on here is that of a unique biographical interest that interprets some of the incidents in legendary fashion but does not recast a single one.

Previously, before he makes known anything of his intention, in fact apparently before it has ripened into a firm decision, he visits his parents in Miedzyborz, which had once been the domicile of Baal-Shem-Tov and where he had spent his own childhood. Here something strange takes place. Once, when he was a boy, he used to run to his great-grandfather's grave at night and ask him to help him to come near to God. But now, when his mother asks him when he intends to depart, he replies: "If my great-grandfather wants to meet me, let him come here." One can detect the fear lest the Baal-Shem, who was prevented "by heaven" when he himself wanted to travel to Palestine, might oppose his intention. But in the night his great-grandfather appears to him and in the morning his mother knows it without his having to tell her. Later he only relates that he learned from the apparition that he was to travel to the city of Kamieniec. Of his sojourn in Kamieniec it is reported that he spent the night alone in the city where Jews were forbidden to live and that thereafter the ban was lifted. He himself said later, whoever knows why the land of Israel was first in the hands of the Canaanites and did not come into Israel's hands until afterwards ("the skin had to precede the fruit," as he says in one of his didactic speeches) also knows why he was in Kamieniec before he traveled into the land of Israel. It was therefore a symbolical action that he stayed the night in the Jewless city, before he set out for the land promised to Israel, and it was precisely this action that he understood the Baal-Shem to have commanded him to perform. Before he set out for Miedzyborz, he had stated that he himself did not know whither he was traveling. By sending him to Kamieniec, his great-grandfather showed him the way he was to go.

On his return home he delivers an exposition on the Psalm verse: "My soul has clung unto Thee, Thy right hand has held me up" (Psalms 63, 9). The exposition has not come down to us, but we can guess the gist of it: He to whom his soul has clung from his childhood days—we know of the boy's tempestuous search for the favor of God—has now stretched forth His hand to support him. But at the same time his little daughter dies, and he connects this too with the new process that has begun; this too is strictly part of the context of the simultaneously wholly factual and wholly symbolical proceedings.

On the even of the Feast of the Passover he says, coming out of the ritual plunge-bath, to his attendant: "In this year I shall certainly be in the Holy Land." The speech which he makes on the Feast is based on the Psalm verse: "Thy way is in the sea, and thy path in the great waters and thy footsteps are not known" (Psalms 77, 19). Now they all know what he has in mind.

His wife tries in vain to persuade him to give up his plan. Who is going to feed his family while he is away? He replies that relations must look after them or they must go and work for strangers. He ignores the weeping all around him: whatever happens, he must travel—his greatest part is already there and the minority must follow the majority. He knows that he will encounter innumerable obstacles, but so long as there is breath in him he will risk his soul and go. At every step of the journey, he recounted later, "I have risked my soul."

In Rabbi Nachman's teaching as it has come down to us from later years we meet the "Obstacles" in connection with Palestine again and again. The obstacles have, according to this teaching, a great significance. They are put in the way of the man whose yearning and destiny impel him into the Holy Land, so that he may overcome them. For they excite and exalt his will and make him worthy to receive the holiness of the land. Whoever intends to be truly Jewish, that is to say, to climb from step to step, must "smash" the obstacles. But in order to conquer in this fight, "holy boldness" is needed, the kind in which God delights, for He praises Israel because of the holy boldness and obstinacy of the Israelite man for the sake of which the Torah was given. This struggle is ultimately a spiritual struggle; for the powers of evil increase the obstacles in order to confuse the understanding, and fundamentally it alone is the source of the obstacles. But the greater a man is, the greater are the obstacles before him, for an all the more intense struggle is demanded of him in order to raise him on to a higher level.

After Nachman had announced his decision he seems to have been besieged with questions as to his reasons. Various answers have come down to us, as for example that he was concerned to amalgamate the commandments that can only be fulfilled in Palestine with the others, and to fulfill them first of all here, in thought, and then there in action; or that, after having now acquired the "lower wisdom" here, he wanted to attain the "higher wisdom" which can only be attained there. But the decisive motive is obviously to establish contact with a holiness which has its sole dwelling-place in Palestine, a contact by which one is enabled and authorized first there, and then here, to do mysterious works and to reach the summit of one's own vocation. In thinking of the greatness of the Holy Land, one must not, he declared to his disciples later, long after his return home, imagine a spiritual essence, something with which it is possible to establish contact here: "I mean," he said, "quite simply this land of Israel with these houses and dwellings." There is an emphatic concreteness of feeling here in Nachman such as we hardly ever find before him. Palestine as a concrete whole is what is meant by the Holy Land. This holiness cannot, however, be perceived from outside. In later years Rabbi Nachman tells of what he heard from famous men who had immigrated only a short while ago. They told him that before they actually got there they had been quite unable to realize that the land of Israel really exists in the world. From everything they had read about its holiness in books they had imagined that it was "a completely different world." But when they came there they saw that the land really does exist in this world, and in its outward appearance it is not different in kind from the other countries from which they had come, its dust is like the dust of the whole world. And yet the land is entirely holy. It is as with the true zaddik who likewise looks exactly like all other men. In truth, however, the land is separate from other lands in every respect and even the sky above it is different from the sky elsewhere. It is as with the true zaddik: only the man who believes in holiness recognizes and receives it.

When all other arguments to persuade Nachman to abandon his decision had failed it was pointed out to him that he had no money for the journey. "I shall travel immediately," he replied, "whatever the conditions, and even without money. Those who take pity on me will give me something." Now that they saw that he was not to be held back, his relations collected the necessary sum of money, and a week after the Feast of the Passover Nachman departed with one attendant. When he was staying the night in a certain place on the Sabbath, Rabbi Mendel of Vitebsk, who had gone to Palestine with three hundred trusty companions twenty years previously and had died there ten years ago, at the beginning of this very month, appeared to him in a dream. As a boy he had even visited the Baal-Shem. Stories about him and his own statements agree in establishing that he continued Baal-Shem's fight against the Messianic fever both before his journey to the Holy Land and in the Holy Land itself. The story is told that when he was staying in Jerusalem a foolish man had, without being noticed, climbed the Mount of Olives and blown on the ram's horn which is the sign for the beginning of the world and said: "There is no renewal." His companion, Rabbi Abraham of Kolisko, gives those who have remained at home information about the many "changes, revolutions, events and time sequences" through which every individual in the land must pass "until he is a real part of it and delights in its stones and feels kindly towards its dust and loves the ruins in the land of Israel ... until the days of his resorption are over and he is fully resorbed into the life . . . . Everyone who comes to the Sanctuary must be born again in his mother's womb, be suckled again, be a little child again and so on, until he looks directly into the face of the land and his soul is bound up with its soul." Rabbi Mendel himself writes to those who have remained at home: "My dear ones, my friends and companions, know truly that I know perfectly clearly that all the sufferings which we have passed through in these three years are the sufferings of the land of Israel," that is to say, they are part of the sufferings which are, according to the Talmudic tradition, necessary in order to acquire the land; they are therefore of precisely the same kind as the "obstacles" which Rabbi Nachman interprets. This is the man, therefore, who appears to him in the first night of his journey. He reveals to him that on a sea voyage the divine name of "Thou" must be called upon: He will overcome the waves, as it is written in the Psalms (89, 10): "Thou rulest the swelling of the sea; when its waves rise, Thou calmest them."

He spends the Feast of the Revelation in Cherson, on the journey to Odessa. A speech which he makes here obviously links up with the communication which he received in the dream; it is based on the Psalm verse: "He maketh the storm a calm so that the waves thereof are still" (Psalms 107, 29). On the eve of the Feast, after his usual vigil, he goes into the plunge-bath with a companion. On the way he asks him time after time whether he cannot hear the sound, the man denies it, finally Nachman says: "It may be coming from a band." But the man understands: The Rabbi has heard the thunder of Sinai.

The sea route via Odessa had hitherto been avoided

by the Jews as dangerous. He undertakes it and from then on it seems safe to everyone. It often happened like this in his life, we are told: he draws the poison-fangs from the things that he is the first to dare to endure.

As soon as the ship is on the high seas, a storm breaks out, water floods the deck. In the great storm Nachman sees a young man coming towards him who had recently died in his home district and hears him entreating him to bring redemption to his soul. That is the first of very many souls who appear to him in this way.

In Istambul troubles and hardships increase. Nachman forbids his companion to say who he is. He not only has to suffer at the hands of the Turkish officials—it is the period of Napoleon's Egyptian expedition, and the fear of spies is great—but he is even suspected and insulted by the Jews; he keeps nevertheless to his disguise, not merely endures the abuse but even provokes it deliberately and contrives to increase it. If, he says to his disciples in a later period, he had not experienced all the humiliation, then he would have remained in Istambul, in other words, he would have had to die there. "Before one achieves greatness," he says, "one must first descend to small-ness. But the land of Israel is the greatest greatness, and that is why one must go down into the smallest smallness before one can rise up to it. That is why the Baal-Shem-Tov was not able to reach there for he was unable to descend to such smallness." But he, Nachman, makes himself small. He goes around in Istambul with bare feet, in a loose coat of coat-lining without a belt, without a hat over his skull cap, and perpetrates all kinds of tomfoolery; thus he organizes with several other people war games in which one side represents the French and the other those attacked by them. This making himself small and acting the fool, which reminds us of Buddhist, Sufic, and Franciscan legends, establishes itself so firmly in him that later on, in Palestine itself, he finds it difficult to get rid of the habit.

In Istambul the plague breaks out. For a long time he is unable to travel on. On account of the approaching danger from the French the Jewish community forbids all indigenous and foreign Jews to leave the city by sea. Nachman resists the prohibition and induces many to travel with him. On the journey a great storm breaks out again and the ship is threatened. All are weeping and praying but he remains seated and silent. People question and press him in vain; at first he makes no reply, then he scolds them: "Keep quiet, all of you! As soon as you are quiet, the sea will also quiet down." And so it happens. After further troubles—the drinking water gives out—the ship comes to Jaffa. Rabbi Nachman intends to go on to Jerusalem from here, for the Holy City is the goal of his desire—he explains explicitly that he does not want to go either to Safed or Tiberias, where the Hasidic groups have settled—but the harbor authorities suspect him, on account of his conspicuous appearance, of being a French spy and forbid him to land. This takes place two days before the high Feast of the New Year. The captain means to stay some days outside Jaffa, but the ship cannot anchor because of the rough sea. In reply to his questions, the wise men of Sephardic Jewry tell the astonished captain that according to an oral tradition the prophet Jonah was once thrown into the sea in this place; this is believed to be the reason why a ship is sometimes prevented from riding at anchor here. They travel on to Haifa and anchor the evening after at the foot of Carmel, opposite the cave of the prophet Elijah. In the morning the prayers are said on the ship, then the Jews go on land, Rabbi Nachman among them.

In later times he tells his disciples that as soon as he had gone four ells in the land, he had already brought about all he had striven for. In this report the belief in the power of *contact* with the holiness of this land becomes particularly clear. What he means is explained by another statement about what he had achieved which he made soon after his return from Palestine and which is to be compared to that on the amalgamation of the commandments which are destined for the Holy Land with the other ones. He said that he had now fulfilled the whole Torah in every way, "for I have attained the fulfillment of the whole Torah, and even if I had been sold to the Ishmaelites in distant lands, where there are no Jews, and had been put there to graze cattle, and even if I had then no longer known the times of the Sabbath and feast days and had no longer had either prayer mantle or prayer strap and not any commandment I could accomplish I should have nevertheless been able to fulfill the whole Torah."

In the afternoon—it is the even of the New Year—they go into the plunge-bath and afterwards into the house of prayer where they stay until the evening. "Blessed art thou," Nachman says to his attendant on his return to the inn, "that thou wast judged worthy to be with me here." He has the names of all the Hasidim read aloud to him, who had joined him at home and had given him slips of paper with their names and the names of their mothers, so that he might remember them in the Holy Land, and he thinks of each one of them in his great joy.

But on the morning after, his feeling has changed. An unspeakable anxiety has been aroused in him, his heart is oppressed and he speaks to no one. Immediately after the feast he thinks of the return journey. He does not even any longer want to go to Jerusalem, he wants to go back to Poland. From Safed and Tiberias come invitations of the zaddikim, who have heard of his arrival, to spend the Feast of the Tabernacle with them but he ignores them and remains for both the Day of Reconciliation and the Feast of the Tabernacle in Haifa.

And now something happens which is indeed not very remarkable in itself, but becomes remarkable through the way in which first Nachman himself, and later his disciples, to whom he relates it, regard it. Day after day a young Arab comes into the inn when the Rabbi is sitting at his midday and evening meal, sits down beside him and keeps on talking to him, kindly but insistently, tapping him on the shoulder between times and showing him his good will in every conceivable way. Nachman naturally does not understand a word of what he is saying, and the demonstrations of love make him pretty uncomfortable, but he does not express any impatience and remains

197

seated as if he were listening. But one day the Arab returns, armed and angry, and marches violently up to the Rabbi who naturally again does not understand a word. Only after the Arab has departed does he learn that he had been challenged to a fight. Nachman is hidden in the home of another zaddik. The Arab comes to the inn again and is beside himself when he hears that the man he is looking for has escaped him. "God knows," he solemnly declares, "that I love him dearly. I want to give him a donkey and my own horse so that he can go to Tiberias with a caravan." Nachman then returns to the inn. The young Arab comes again, but now says not a word, he merely smiles at the Rabbi from time to time. Apparently he also fulfills his promise. Evidently he was only concerned to hire the animals—we can explain the happenings related in this way—and as the Rabbi appeared to listen to him, he felt offended because he did not accept his often repeated offer; in the end the situation was cleared up and when he looked at Nachman he had to laugh. In a statement that has come down to us, the Rabbi said that he had suffered more from the Arab's love than from his anger. But beyond that he seems to have dropped a few hints about the mysterious danger that lay behind this episode, and the pupils understood him to mean that the Arab had been Satan in person. We here gain a particular insight into the symbolically legendary way in which Nachman experiences his life and in which his disciples learn of it from his report and work it up into the story that has come down to us. The Arabian donkey-hirer becomes the Satanic embodiment of the "obstacles." This is given as the explanation of the melancholy that the Rabbi experienced before the conflict.

Meanwhile Nachman allows himself to be persuaded to undertake the journey to Tiberias, where he falls ill—once again an event of symbolical significance. Then we hear of an informer whose designs he frustrates. Visits to some caves of holy men are reported with a few legendary touches. Thus he is said to have visited a cave with the tomb of a holy child, which had hitherto been shunned on account of a snake that was supposed to reside there; when he came, no snake was there, and from then on everybody visited the cave. Here too Nachman appears as the forerunner, the pioneer.

One of the great Jews of Tiberias presses him to reveal to him the hidden purpose of his coming to Palestine. Obviously, he said, the Rabbi was concerned to perform a secret action in the service of God; if he would only tell him what it was he would assist him to the limit of his powers. When Nachman refuses, he asks him to make known something of his teaching to him. But as soon as he begins to tell him the secret of the four points of the compass in the land of Israel, blood rushes out of his throat and he has to break off, for "heaven does not agree."

In Tiberias the plague breaks out. Nachman makes his way on subterranean paths through a cave and not without danger, to Safed. Attempting to find place on a ship for the return journey, he comes with his attendant on to a Turkish warship, which they take for a merchantman. They discover their mistake too late. After undergoing severe hardships and all kinds of adventures they reach Rhodes where they celebrate the Feast of the Passover. From there they travel by way of Istambul and Wallachia. Here the Rabbi speaks on the Sabbath at the holy Third Meal about the verse of the prophet Isaiah: "When thou passest through the waters—I [ = I am] with thee" (43,2). This speech closes, in the version that has come down to us, with the words: "I with thee—see that thou becomest the tool that is called I." This is what he wants to declare of himself in this hour: that on his journey over the water he has become the tool called I.

This enables us to understand what he henceforth,

in the time—not much more than a decade—which still remained of his life and in which he built up his teaching and writing, reports to his disciples again and again, if only in hint, of what he had acquired in the Holy Land. Thus he relates that before the "six hundred thousand" letters of the Torah surrounded him as if the Torah had broken up again into an uncontrolled profusion of letters; but since Palestine this disturbance has ceased and he has the whole of it in his mind in such a way that it is impossible for it to split up and become chaotic. Or: in his youth he was often overcome by violent tempers and he fought against them; but to break a bad habit does not mean that it has been completely overcome; on the contrary, the whole force of the passion at work in it must be transformed into good: he had only succeeded in this—no longer merely not hating, but loving what previously seemed hateful with all the passionateness that had previously gone into the hatred—in the land of Israel. And the same is true of the teaching. Between the doctrines which come from outside Palestine and those which come from Palestine, he says, there is a difference as great as that dividing East and West.

Statements that he made nine weeks before his death on the eve of the Sabbath after the Mourning on the Ninth day of the month Ab, the day of the destruction of the Temple, give an even deeper insight into the transformation that he owed to the land. Shortly before, he had moved into a new house, his last, where he looked out from the window on to a garden and, beyond that, the cemetery—with the graves of the thousands who had perished in the great Cossack massacre; he looked at it again and again and said how good it would be to lie among the martyrs. This was the first discourse in the new house. Many Hasidim, from long-standing intimates to those who had only just joined him, were gathered together as he entered and performed the consecration of the wine. It was obvious that he was very weak and hardly had the strength to speak. Afterwards he did not return to his room as was his usual custom, but remained seated at the table. Very feebly he began to speak. "Why do you come to see me?" he said, "I know nothing now, I am now a simpleton." This he repeated time and again. But then he added that he was only holding on to life because he had been in the land of Israel. And as soon as he had said this, his teaching power arose within him again, the enthusiasm overcame him, and he began to speak of the fact that vital force flows into all the simpletons in the world from the zaddik's condition of simplicity, for everything is interconnected. But the source of this vital force is in the land that was the land of grace even before Israel entered it with the revelation of the Torah, the "treasury of the undeserved gift." It was from here that the world was preserved between Creation and Revelation, here the doctrine of God was hidden, the Ten Words of Sinai in the Ten Words with which the world was created, and this is the teaching in which the fathers lived in the land. It is called Derekh Erets, "the way of the earth," in other words, the right way of life outside Revelation, and indeed it is the way to the earth, to the land. Since the power of the Ten Words of Creation is hidden in the land and the fathers have lived in the strength of the Ten Words, Israel, to whom God "proclaimed the power of His works," as "to His own people," was able to come into the land with the Ten Words revealed to them. Thus Israel's appropriation of the land is the encounter and association of Creation and Revelation. In order to prepare the way for it, Canaan first had to be in the hands of the heathen, before it fell to the lot of Israel; but that is precisely why the peoples cannot say to Israel: "Ye are robbers, in that ye have conquered a land that does not belong to you." Admittedly this is only so as long as Israel merits this exceptional consideration, so long as it hallows the created earth with the holiness of the revealed Torah which it fulfills and is allowed to remain in its land; as soon as Israel has to go into exile, the land enters once again into the state of the hidden doctrine, of the Ten Words of Creation alone, of the undeserved gift, of pure grace. The zaddik lives on this strength of the land when he falls into the state of simplicity and from there the vital force streams into him which flows from him to all the simple-minded in the world, not only of Israel but of all peoples. This is precisely why he has occasionally to fall for a time into this state of simplicity. Thus even in the deepest sinking there is the hidden purpose of an ultimate rising. And thus it is in some measure and some way for all men, for the men of spirit as well as the simple: from none is the source of life with-held unless he himself withdraws from it. Therefore the most important thing is not to despair. "There is no such thing as despair!" cried Rabbi Nachman. "One must not despair! I implore you, do not des-pair!" A great joy had been kindled within him. Be-fore they washed their hands before the meal he bid them strike up the song, "I will sing praises," that was not usually sung until after the blessing, and had not been sung at all since he had become so weak. "Strike it up, Naftali," he said to a pupil. When the latter blushed and hesitated, he cried: "Why should we be ashamed? The whole world was created for our sake! Naftali, why should we be ashamed?" And he himself joined in the singing. "Thus we have seen," the disciple writes in his narrative, "how God's concealment is transformed into grace. From a state of ignorance the Rabbi has arrived at such a revelation. He himself said that his ignorance was more remarkable than his knowledge."

Rabbi Nachman did not travel to Palestine for a second time. Three years before his death he said that he had wanted to go there to die, but he had been afraid that he might die on the way and then no one would come to his grave and tend it. "I want," he said on another occasion, "to remain among you." But Palestine permeated everything in his mind. "My place," he used to say, "is only the land of Israel. If I travel anywhere I shall travel only to the land of Israel."

When he spoke of the holiness of the land, he sometimes fell into such deep ecstasy that he came near to dying.

Rabbi Nachman of Bratzlav is one of those Hasidim who, like Rabbi Mendel of Vitebsk and his companions, hint at the resettlement of the land by their own settlement in Palestine. In this respect he does

205

not, as in the fairy tales he told, introduce a new era.
But as the great heir that he is, he melted down all
the traditional material into his glorification of the
holiness of the land and reshaped it. No one in the
whole of Jewish literature has ever praised it so mani-
foldly and so uniformly at the same time.

According to Rabbi Nachman, Palestine is the
starting point of the creation of the world, its founda-
tion stone, and it is the source of the coming world
in which everything will be good. It is the real center
of the spirit of life and therefore the renewal of the
world by the spirit of life will also proceed from it.
The spring of joy, the perfection of wisdom and the
music of the world is in it. It represents the covenant
between heaven and earth. The perfecting of faith
proceeds from it, for here one can give oneself up
wholly to the infinite light as nowhere else in the
world and be illuminated by it; from it there proceeds the setting right and perfecting of justice in the
world, and the overcoming of anger and cruelty. It
is the place of peace in which the antitheses of grace
and power are united and the unity of God is revealed; it is here that peace is established in the human
heart, "between his bones," between man and man,
and from here peace goes out into the world. Rabbi
Nachman adopts the Talmudic teaching that all other

lands receive the heavenly plenty through messengers, through the "princes of the upper sphere," but that Israel receives it directly from the hands of God Himself: that is why it is so difficult for the other peoples to advance to unity, whereas Israel is embraced as a unity by the dictum "Thou art one" and from Israel unity is to come over the whole world of man. Therefore the land of Israel is as it were the Shekhina, the "indwelling" of God Himself.

The land is the highest of all lands, but it is also the lowest of all. Canaan means "submission," as it is written: "And the humble shall inherit the land." The highest land submits itself in the deepest humility and its very dust teaches the lesson of humility. Therefore the resurrection of the dead will have its center here. But for the same reason Israel has not yet regained the land. "Because of pride we have not yet returned to the land." It is particularly stressed that it is not because the others are so many but on account of their own ambition and haughtiness that the Jews cannot get back to their land. The obstacle is in themselves.

But the dust of the land of Israel has a "magnetic" power too: it draws men to holiness. There are two opposite kinds and powers of dust: the dust of the land of Israel, which attracts men to holiness, and an impure counter-dust which attracts them to the "Other Side." But this "counter-dust" takes on the same appearance as the pure dust and behaves as if it were the dust that attracts men to holiness. "For in this world everything is mixed up and confused." But in reality it is nothing but an ensnaring and entangling constraining power. This is the "dust of the Other Side." In the language of today: the power of the earth over man is twofold. The earth can exert a healing influence on the man who settles on it and serves it, by binding him to its indwelling holiness, and then the spirit of man is supported, strengthened and borne by the power of the earth; but it can also pull man down and stir up his powers of imagination against the spirit; it can deny and renounce the higher powers and assign all power to itself. In the nature of the earth as everywhere in the world, purity and impurity, consecrating and desecrating influences confront each other. But the pure and healing power of the earth is represented in the land of Israel.

We have heard that the resurrection of the dead will have its center in the land of Israel. That is why the tomb achieves its perfect form here; here alone is the place of perfect burial. For the reason why death has been imposed on man is known to tradition: it is because in the sin of the first man a defilement by the serpent invaded our imagination from which we can be perfectly cleansed in no other way than by the death of the body. In a proper death and a proper burial the impurity is dissolved and a new body will arise in a renewed world. All this, however, is perfectly achieved only in the land of Israel. For the overcoming of the defiled imagination occurs through faith, but the power of faith has implanted itself in this land and lives and works therein. Abraham, the father of faith, was the first to reveal this holy power when he acquired the burial place of the cave of Makhpela.

Here, in the land of Israel, the purification of the imagination through faith takes place. It is not for nothing that the sounds of the words *adama*, soil, and *medame*, imagination, resemble one another: the fullness of the elements comes to the imagination from the earth. But the purification of the imagination by faith can also take place in no other way than through the consecrated earth and the consecrated earth is here, in the land of Israel. Everywhere else the sparks of faith have fallen into the confused imagination which is overlaid by the earth. Therefore it is already written of the fathers (Exodus 13, 17) that "God led them not through the way of the land of the Philistines, although that was near," but "God led the

people about": in order that they might take care of
the sparks of faith dwelling everywhere and to purify
the imagination in all the places through which they
pass. In this way a man becomes worthy of receiving
the perfection of the purified imagination and the
perfection of faith in the land of Israel.

All this, however, both the significance of the holiness of the land and the difficulties which rise up before the man who really wants to attain it, must be
grasped at a still deeper level.

Because here in the land of Israel faith has the place
of its perfection, because here in very truth is "the
gate of heaven," in which the upper and lower spheres
meet and one can enter here from the outside into
the inside and those who stand outside can join up
with those inside, hence "the perfection of all worlds
and the perfection of all souls" proceeds from here.
For this perfection develops from man's utter sur-
render to the light of the boundless, but this can only
happen here, nowhere else can man receive and
absorb the light with his whole nature. For this to
come about, however, it is necessary that the vessels
shall first be perfected in order to receive the light.
And again only the holiness of the land can bring
about the perfection of the vessels. That is why it is
so difficult to get there for those who want to attain

the holiness of the land. The former depends on the latter and the latter on the former. How is one to get out of this vicious circle? The greater the one, the greater the obstacles. That is why whoever stakes his soul to reach the land, breaks through the vicious circle, for the light of the holiness of the land streams towards those who still stand outside and gives them the strength to break the obstacles, the demonic "shell-powers." The vessel is perfected and gives itself up, service in the cause of the perfection of all worlds and all souls takes place.

When the sons of Israel adopted the Torah and came into the land, they were allowed to raise its holiness from obscurity into the light of day. When they transgressed against its manifest holiness, by not fulfilling what was revealed to them, and finally had to leave the land, its holiness fell back into obscurity again and has lived and worked there ever since. "The land of Israel still continues in its holiness out of the power of the hidden Torah and undeserved grace. And therefore we are always on the lookout for a chance to return to our land. For we know: although it is in great seclusion the land is still ours even now."

Even though the "other side" has robbed Israel of its land, it proclaims its protest in the power of prayer. It cries: "The land is ours, for it is our inheritance." And so long as it proclaims its claim to the land, according to divine law the appropriation of the land by the "other side" is no authentic appropriation. But how is the land to be regained? Everyone from Israel has a share in the land, everyone from Israel can have a share in its redemption. According to the measure in which he purifies and sanctifies himself, so he will be judged worthy to seize and conquer a part of the land. The holiness of the land can only be conquered gradually. But since this part must take place in the whole of life, in every action and in every domain, it is right that man should withdraw from the learning of the Torah from time to time and concern himself with the "way of the earth," as the wise men say.

Those, however, who have been judged worthy to settle in the land of Israel, are to remember at all times the great radiance and illumination that went forth from the land in early times and are to remember that holiness is eternal. And even when its illuminating power seems to have disappeared, a holy trace of it remains. With its eyes fixed thereon, Israel hopes and waits at all times for a "new light to shine on Zion."

This land is a small, humiliated land—yet the hope of the world is contained within it. Whoever settles

212

in it in truth, so that he has intercourse with the holiness of the land and helps it to prepare the way for the redemption of the world, into his apparently poverty-stricken life there streams the glory of the higher spheres, yearning for union with the lower. He eats "bread with salt," as recommended by the wise men as "the Way of the Instruction," but this bread is in fact the very bread of the land and the grace of faith is harvested, ground, and baked into it. "In the land of Israel the bread is so tasty that it contains all the pleasant taste of all the foods in the world. As is written: 'Thou shalt not eat thy bread in indigence, it shall not lack anything.'"

In one of his tales Rabbi Nachman tells of a simple shoemaker who eats dry bread for his midday meal, first as a spicy soup, then as a juicy roast and who ends by enjoying it as a delightful cake: he lacks nothing. Does his imagination deceive him as to the poverty of his existence or does his faith not rather enable him to taste in the divine food what lies hidden therein? Nachman, who like all genuine masters of the Hasidic doctrine praises the wisdom of simplicity again and again, points out that the patriarch Jacob who was given the land of Canaan for his own (he is the real receiver among the patriarchs, because none of his sons must be excluded but together they already represent the people of Israel), is called a "simple man." Of the land of Israel itself Rabbi Nachman says that it represents simplicity. That means, however, that it represents the true wisdom. For it is the true wisdom to taste in one's bread all the pleasant tastes of the world and it is the true wisdom to recognize the gate of heaven in the poor and sterile little land.

# APPENDIX

The following thirteen "sayings" (**Lehrworte**) of Rabbi Nachman were found among the Buber's papers deposited in the Martin Buber Archive at the University and National Library in Jerusalem. Each saying is recorded on a separate sheet of paper. At the bottom of each translation, Buber noted the original Hebrew source from which the text was taken. All thirteen "sayings" are from *Likkute Mo-HaRan* (LM. 1808; 1811), a two volume Hebrew compilation of Rabbi Nachman's teachings. The "sayings" here have been translated from the German by Elizabeth Petuchowski.

## Sayings of Rabbi Nachman

### The Judgment

Whoever seeks knowledge of the hidden light, must raise the status of fear up to the level of its origin. This is achieved by judging oneself and all one's strivings and doings. This way, a man sheds all his anxieties and raises up the fallen fear. But if he does not judge himself, he will be judged from above, and the judgment clothes itself in all things, and all things in the world turn into messengers of God, to execute judgment upon this man.

LM I, 15:1–2

# Body and Soul

Each man should have pity on his own body and should let it have a portion of every enlightenment received by the soul. He should thoroughly purify his body, so that it can have a portion of everything which the soul receives, in order that matters no longer stand as before, namely that your soul achieves loftiness while your body knows nothing of this. And if your body has its portion, then the soul, in turn, may benefit. For at times, the soul falls off its rung, and then the purified body can help raise it up again with the power of the light which it has absorbed. Therefore Job says: "While in my flesh, I behold God" [Job 19:26].

LM I 22:5

# Life

There is no difference between life and death, unless it be this: that now one dwells here, and then in the grave. True life, that is: eternal life is God's alone, for He lives eternally. And he who is rooted in Him lives likewise eternally, for he is one with Him.

LM I 21:9

# The Revealed and the Concealed

Two things Israel said at Mount Horeb: "We will do and we will hear" [Exodus 24:7].[1] These two are: the revealed — namely the law and the commandment, that which can and should be done — and the concealed which surrounds the

*216*

law and the commandment without entering them, of which one knows only in prayer, as it is said: "You have given your servant a hearing [discerning] heart" [1 Kings 3:9], only in prayer while one clings to what is boundless. These two are found in every world; each man has both, each according to his rung. And whoever ascends to a higher rung, has his "We hear" changed to "We do" and then receives a new "We hear," and so from rung to rung. And it is the same with the worlds: What is a "We hear" for our world, is a "We do" for the world of the heavenly spheres, and they have a higher "We hear," and so from world to world.

LM I 22:9

## Hints

This whole world is the clothing of the lowest rungs of holiness, of its feet, as it were. At it is written: "The earth is the footstool unto My feet" [Isaiah 66:1]. God limits his divine nature from infinity to the center of the material world, where the human being stands. And He joins each human being to thought, word and deed, according to the day and place and person, and He clothes therein hints how to bring him close to His service. Therefore, every human being should steep himself in trying to understand the hints clothed for him in thought, word and deed, uniquely for him, in matters of his work and his business affairs, everything just as God joins day to day.

LM I 54:2

# How God Conceals Himself

There are two ways of concealing oneself. One is that God, indeed, conceals Himself, so that it is very hard to find Him, and yet a man who knows that God is hiding from him, can forge ahead and find Him. The other way is for God to conceal that he is concealing Himself, so that a man truly does not know of God and therefore cannot find Him. That is of which it is written: "Conceal will I, conceal" [cf. Deut 31:18]. Then God conceals His concealment, and those from whom He conceals it, do not know Him who is Concealed.

LM I 56:3

# Human Creation

Know that the conflict of opinions resembles the creation of the world. For essential in the creation of the world is a certain cleared area: without it, there would have been no room for the creation of a world. Therefore God confined the light to the edges, so that an area became clear, and into that He created all of creation through His word. As it is written: "Through the word of the Lord, the heavens were made" [Psalm 33:6]. And this is also the way in which conflicts of opinions work. For in a world containing only one single wise man, no creation would happen. Only because opinions are divided and each one pulls in a different direction, a free area, as it were, becomes cleared and into that, creation happens through the Word. For all words spoken in conflicting opinions are only for the sake of the creation of the world, which happens through them in the free space between them.

LM I 64:4

## The Great Holiness

There is a great Tzaddik, so great that the world cannot abide his holiness. That is why he very much conceals himself, without any particular sanctity or reclusiveness being apparent. That is similar to the Song of Songs of which it is said: "All songs are a sanctuary, but the Song of Songs is the holy of holies" [Mishnah Yadayim 3:5]. King Solomon, peace be upon him, authored three books. Two of them, Proverbs and Ecclesiastes, are full of moral teachings and the fear of God, and they contain frequent mention of purity and piety, but the Song of Songs shuns such words. Because of the great power of its holiness, no kind of holiness meets the eye.

LM I 243

## Sorrow and Joy

At times, when people are joyful and dance, they will seize one who sits apart in his sorrow. They drag him into their dancing round and compel him to be happy with them. This is also what happens in the heart of a person who is joyful: sadness and sorrow withdraw on the sidelines, but it is reckoned as a special virtue to round them up boldly and to bring sadness along into joy, so that all the power of sorrow be changed to joy.

LM II 23

# A Great Advantage

It is a great advantage if one still has an evil inclination. For then one can serve God with the evil inclination itself, that is to say: one can bring forward the whole flame and all the fervor, and offer them in the service of God. But if one has no evil inclination, he also has no complete service. It is essential in the hour of desire to hold back the fervor and to bring it out in the hour of prayer and of service.

LM II 49

# Whoever Has A Heart

Whoever has a heart is indifferent to space and, place, moreover he himself is rather the place of the world. For the divine is in the heart, as it is said in the Psalm: "Rock of my heart!" [Psalm 73:26] And God says to Moses: "See, there is a place [*makom*] near Me" [Exodus 33:21]. For God, as we know, is the place [*makom*] of the world, the world is not his place.[2] And so it is with the person who has a heart, because the deity is in the heart. It does not behove one with the heart of an Israelite to say: "This place does not suit me." For place and space should not matter to him, because he is the place [*makom*] of the world, the world is not his place.

LM II 56

## Above Time

Human understanding cannot grasp that God is above time. But know, that time exists only because we do not understand, because our understanding is little. For the greater our understanding, the more does time vanish. In a dream we live through seventy years and realize, upon waking, that it was a quarter of an hour. In this waking dream of our life, we live through seventy years and awaken to a higher understanding where we become aware that it was a quarter of an hour. We can never grasp with our lower understanding what we will notice with our higher understanding. But perfect understanding is above time.

After the Messiah has experienced what he has experienced since the creation of the world, and has suffered what he has suffered, God says to him: "You are my son, and I have fathered you this day" [Psalm 2:7].

LM II 61

## Inner Turmoil

It is very good to confer in solitude and stillness with one's creator, to recite Psalms to him and prayers of supplication with a whole heart until one is overcome with weeping so that one weeps to God like a child to its father. But to be occupied in prayer with the purpose of weeping, is not a good undertaking. For now, he can no longer say whatever he says with his whole heart, and great, true weeping will no longer stir up in him. Moreover, thoughts about prayer belong to the realm of the "strange thoughts," which prevent the soul's complete turning towards God.

LM II 95

# NOTES

1. The key-term in this Scriptual passage, *nishma*, is usually rendered, "we shall obey." Following Rabbi Nachman's homiletical intent and that of other traditional Jewish exegetes, Buber translated the term literally, "we shall hear."

2. "The Place" (*Ha-Makom*) is a traditional appelation for God.